VOGUE® KNITTING
STITCHIONARY® 6

The Ultimate Stitch Dictionary from the Editors of Vogue® Knitting Magazine

volume six
edgings

VOGUE® KNITTING

STITCHIONARY® 6

The Ultimate Stitch Dictionary from the Editors of Vogue® Knitting Magazine

volume six
edgings

sixth&spring books

sixth&spring books

161 Avenue of the Americas
Suite 1301
New York, New York 10013

Executive Editor
Carla Scott

Managing Editor
Wendy Williams

Senior Editor
Michelle Bredeson

Art Director
Diane Lamphron

Book Design
Chi Ling Moy

Yarn Editor
Renée Lorion

Technical Editor
Charlotte Parry

Technical Illustrations
Charlotte Parry
Uli Monch

Vice President, Publisher
Trisha Malcolm

Production Manager
David Joinnides

Creative Director
Joe Vior

President
Art Joinnides

1   3   5   7   9   10   8   6   4   2
Manufactured in China
First Edition

Library of Congress Control Number: 2011931160
ISBN: 978-1-936096-22-0

The patterns for the garments shown on the following pages are available for purchase at vogueknitting.com:
Page 9: Surplice Wrap Top, *Vogue Knitting,* Spring/Summer 2002
Page 23: Shrug, *Vogue Knitting,* Winter 2006/2007
Page 41: Cardigan, *Vogue Knitting,* Fall 2006
Page 65: Cropped Jacket, *Vogue Knitting,* Spring/Summer 2005
Page 101: Pullover, *Vogue Knitting,* Fall 2005
Page 127: Jacket, *Vogue Knitting,* Winter 2002/2003
Page 141: Flower-Edged Scarf, *Vogue Knitting,* Fall 2002

contents

We dedicate this book to all the wonderfully skilled knitters who spent their days (and nights) creating the beautiful swatches that appear in this book.

It's hard to believe this is the sixth installment in the STITCHIONARY series. Originally conceived as a three-volume series, it has grown beyond our expectations. Once we started to go through the archives and realized how much material we had to choose from, it seemed only natural to continue. The warm reception we have received from knitters and crocheters confirmed our decision. The first five volumes covered knit and purl stitches, cables, colorwork, crochet and lace. With STITCHIONARY 6: EDGINGS, we are bringing all of these techniques together in one volume.

As for all of the STITCHIONARY titles, we created this collection by poring through the VOGUE KNITTING archives. We narrowed down patterns from thousands of designs from the magazine to bring you the very best examples of edgings. The edgings range from narrow and discreet trims to voluptuous showstoppers and everything in between. There is no easier way to customize a design than by changing its edging. Edgings can be used to embellish hems, cuffs, necklines, pockets and front bands of cardigans. You don't have to use just one in a garment—feel free to try mixing up ribbed and cabled edgings, for example. Knitting them in the same yarn and color is one way to unify them. Because they are generally small (with exceptions!), knitting and crocheting edgings is a great way to try out new techniques and stretch your skills.

There are a number of ways to incorporate edgings into knitted garments, depending on the edging and your preference: You can knit the edging first and then continue knitting the body or sleeves of the garment. You can pick up stitches along the edge of a garment and knit (or crochet) the edging. You can knit (or crochet) the edging separately and sew it onto the garment. Or you can leave "live" stitches on the edge of the garment and knit or graft the edging to it.

We've divided the 200-plus edgings patterns in this book into seven chapters. "Ribs" features knit and purl stitches that combine to create stretchy vertical ribbed or horizontal fabrics perfect for cuffs and hems. The patterns in "Texture" range from delicate picot trims to rich, frothy ruffles. In the "Cables" chapter, braids and twists of all types take center stage. Some of the most traditional types of edgings as well as fresh, new designs are featured in "Lace," Stripes, Fair Isle designs, intarsia motifs, slip-stitch patterns and more take edgings in new directions in "Color," In "Unusual," you will find patterns that incorporate fringe, beads, embroidery and other embellishments. Finally, crocheters will find plenty of patterns to sink their hooks into in "Crochet."

Carla Scott

grecian formula p. 53

how to use this book

VOGUE KNITTING STITCHIONARY, VOLUME 6: EDGINGS is divided into seven chapters: Ribs, Texture, Cables, Lace, Color, Unusual and Crochet. As in the previous editions, we arranged the stitches in each chapter in order of difficulty, from the easiest to the most challenging. In naming some swatches we used the most commonly recognized or descriptive names, while for others we just had fun in determining a title.

Depending on the chapter, we have used written instructions, charts or both to explain each stitch. All of the instructions use the VOGUE KNITTING style, with standard knitting abbreviations, easy-to-understand terminology and the internationally recognized stitch symbols for the charts. References to special techniques used in the stitch, such as cables, are spelled out at the beginning of each set of instructions, so you do not have to flip back to a glossary to find the meaning.

We knit the swatches using several yarns from Cascade Yarns. The swatches in the "Ribs" chapter were knit in 220 Sport, "Cables" in Greenland, "Lace" in Heritage, and "Texture," "Color," "Unusual" and "Crochet" in 220 Superwash. For most of the swatches, we used a background of stockinette stitches, which are not included in the instructions. We used sizes 5 (3.75mm) and 6 (4mm) needles to knit the swatches in "Ribs," size 6 for "Lace," size 9 (5.5mm) for "Cables" and sizes 6 and 7 (4.5mm) for the rest. We used a size G/6 (4mm) hook to create the "Crochet" swatches. Note that if you use a different weight of yarn, textured yarn or different-sized needles, the resulting look of the stitch may be different from what we show.

Always remember to make a gauge swatch with the yarn you are using for the project. This will help to familiarize you with the pattern stitch, and you will know if that particular stitch works well with the desired yarn.

ribs

1 k2, p2 rib

(multiple of 4 sts)
Row 1 Knit.
Row 2 *P2, k2; rep from * to end.
Rep rows 1 and 2.

2 k2, p3 rib

(multiple of 5 sts plus 3)
Row 1 (WS) Purl.
Row 2 P3, *k2, p3; rep from * to end.
Rep rows 1 and 2.

1

2

3 k4, p4 rib

(multiple of 8 sts)
Row 1 (RS) *K4, p4; rep from * to end.
Row 2 Purl.
Rep rows 1 and 2.

4 subtle stripes

(multiple of 5 sts plus 2)
Row 1 (RS) K3, *p1, k4; rep from * to last 4 sts,
end p1, k3.
Row 2 K the knit sts and p the purl sts.
Rep rows 1 and 2.

3

4

5 between the rows

(worked over any number of sts)
Row 1 (RS) Knit.
Rows 2–5 Knit.
Row 6 K2, p to last 2 sts, k2.
Rep rows 1–6 for rib.

6 ridges

(worked over any number of sts)
Rows 1, 3, 4 and 6 Purl.
Rows 2 and 5 Knit.
Rep rows 1–6.

5

6

7 checks mix

(multiple of 4 sts plus 2)
Row 1 (RS) *K1, p1; rep from * to end.
Row 2 *K3, p1; rep from * end k2.
Row 3 P2, *k1, p3; rep from * to end.
Row 4 Rep row 1.
Row 5 *K1, p3; rep from * end last rep p1.
Row 6 K1, p1, *k3, p1; rep from * to end.
Rep rows 1–6 for rib.

8 two to three

(beg as a multiple of 4 sts plus 2 and end as a multiple of 6 sts plus 3)
Row 1 (RS) *K2, p2; rep from * end k2.
Row 2 *P2, k2; rep from * end p2.
Rep these 2 rows for 2"/5cm.
K next row and inc 3 sts evenly spaced.
Row 1 (WS) *P3, k3; rep from * end p3.
Row 2 *K3, p3; rep from * end k3.
Rep these 2 rows for 3"/7.5cm more.

ribs

7

8

9 textured rib

(multiple of 5 sts plus 2)
Row 1 (RS) P2, *k3, p2; rep from * to end.
Row 2 K2, *p1, k1, p1, k2; rep from * to end.
Rep rows 1 and 2.

10 wave rib

(worked over 42 sts)
Row 1 (RS) *P1, k1; rep from * to end.
Row 2 *P1, k1; rep from * to end.
Rows 3 to 10 Rep rows 1 and 2.
Row 11 *[P1, k1] 10 times, p1, k5, [p1, k1] 8 times; rep from * to end.
Row 12 *[P1, k1] 7 times, p9, [k1, p1] 9 times, k1; rep from * to end.
Row 13 *[P1, k1] 8 times, p1, k13, [p1, k1] 6 times; rep from * to end.
Row 14 *[P1, k1] 5 times, p17, [k1, p1] 7 times, k1; rep from * to end.
Row 15 *[P1, k1] 6 times, p1, k21, [p1, k1] 4 times; rep from * to end.
Row 16 *[P1, k1] 3 times, p25, [k1, p1] 5 times, k1; rep from * to end.
Row 17 *[P1, k1] 4 times, p1, k29, [p1, k1] twice; rep from * to end.
Row 18 *P1, k1, p33, [k1, p1] 3 times, k1; rep from * to end.
Row 19 *[P1, k1] twice, p1, k37; rep from * to end.

9

10

11 corrugated cardboard

(worked over 21 sts)

Note Sts for St st were picked up after edging was knit.

Row 1 (RS) P1, *k1 tbl, p1; rep from * to end.

Row 2 K the knit sts, p the purl sts tbl.

Rep rows 1 and 2.

12 plaited rib

Psso Pass the sl st over the k1 and yo.

(multiple of 5 sts plus 3)

Row 1 (RS) K3, *sl 1 purlwise, k1, yo, psso, k1, p1, k1; rep from *, end last rep k3.

Row 2 P6, *k1, p4; rep from *, end last rep p6.

Rep rows 1 and 2.

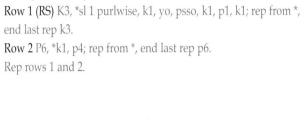

11

12

13 block by block

(worked over 12 sts)

Note Sts for St st were picked up after edging was knit.

Cast on 12 sts.

Work 7 rows in garter st, *beg with a RS row, work 9 rows in St st; 11 rows in garter st; rep from * 7 times more, end last rep 7 rows garter st.

14 placket rib

(multiple of 23 sts plus 10)

Row 1 (RS) K10, P13, k10: rep from * to end.

Row 2 P10, *K13, p10; rep from * to end.

Rows 3–5 Rep rows 1 and 2.

Row 6 (WS) P9, *p2tog, k11, p2tog tbl, p8; rep from *, end last rep p9 instead of p8.

Row 7 K the knit sts and p the purl sts.

Row 8 P9, *p2tog, k9, p2tog tbl, p8; rep from *,

end last rep p9 instead of p8.

Row 9 K the knit sts and p the purl sts.

Row 10 P9, *p2tog, k7, p2tog tbl, p8; rep from *, end last rep p9 instead of p8.

13

14

15 slipped rib

(multiple of 22 sts plus 11)
Note Slip all sts on row 2 wyib.
Row 1 (WS) *[P1, k4] 3 times, p3, k4; rep from *, end [p1, k4] twice, p1.
Row 2 Sl 1, [p4, sl 1] twice, *p4, k1, sl 1, k1, [p4, sl 1] 3 times; rep from * to end.
Rep rows 1 and 2.

16 slipped rib II

(multiple of 6 plus 3)
Row 1 (RS) P3, *k1, k1 wrapping st twice, k1, p3; rep from * to end.
Row 2 *K3, p1, sl 1 wyif dropping the extra wrap, p1; rep from *, end k3.
Row 3 P3, *k1, sl 1 wyib, k1, p3; rep from * to end.
Row 4 *K3, p1, sl 1 wyif, p1; rep from *, end k3.
Rep rows 1–4.

ribs

15

16

17 faux cabled rib

(multiple of 5 sts plus 2)
Row 1 (RS) *P2, k3; rep from * to last 2 sts, p2.
Row 2 *K2, p3; rep from * to last 2 sts, end k2.
Row 3 *P2, wyib sl 1, k2, psso; rep from * to last 2 sts, p2.
Row 4 *K2, p1, yo, p1; rep from * to last 2 sts, k2.
Rep rows 1–4.

18 tiny twisters

(multiple of 9 sts plus 1)
Row 1 K1, *p2, k3, p2, k2; rep from * to end.
Row 2 P2, *k2, p3, k2, p2; rep from *, end last rep p1.
Row 3 K1, *p2, SK2P, p2, k2; rep from * to end.
Row 4 P2, *k2, (p1, k1, p1) in same st, k2, p2; rep from *,
end last rep p1.
Rep rows 1–4.

17

18

19 twist rib

(multiple of 2 sts plus 1)
Row 1 (WS) P1, *k1, p1 tbl; rep from *, end k1, p1.
Row 2 K1, p1, *k1 tbl, p1; rep from *, end k1.
Rep rows 1 and 2.

20 ruffled rib

(multiple of 6 sts plus 3)
Rows 1 and 3 (WS) P3, *k3, p3; rep from * to end.
Row 2 K3, *p3, k3; rep from * to end.
Row 4 K2, *k2tog, yo, p1, yo, ssk, k1; rep from *,
end k1.
Row 5 P3, *k3, p3; rep from * to end.

ribs

19

20

21 zigzag rib

2-st LPC Sl 1 to cn and hold to *front*, p1, k1 tbl from cn.

2-st RPC Sl 1 to cn and hold to *back*, k1 tbl, p1 from cn.

(multiple of 7 sts)

Row 1 *K4, k1 tbl, p2; rep from * to end.

Row 2 *K2, p1 tbl, p4; rep from * to end.

Row 3 *K4, 2-st LPC, p1; rep from * to end.

Row 4 *K1, p1 tbl, k1, p4; rep from * to end.

Row 5 *K4, p1, 2-st LPC; rep from * to end.

Row 6 *P1 tbl, k2, p4; rep from * to end.

Row 7 *K4, p1, 2-st RPC; rep from * to end.

Row 8 *K1, p1 tbl, k1, p4; rep from * to end.

Row 9 *K4, 2-st RPC, p1; rep from * to end.

Rep rows 2–9.

22 alternating twists

Tw2R Knit into front of second st on LH needle, then knit into first st, slipping both sts off needle together.

(multiple of 8 sts plus 2)

Row 1 (RS) K2, *p2, Tw2R, p2, k2; rep from 8 to end.

Row 2 P2, *k2, p2; rep from * to end.

Rep rows 1 and 2.

23 bobble rib

Make Bobble (MB) In st, k into [front, back] twice, then front (5 sts); [turn, sl 1, p4; turn, sl 1, k4] twice; turn, pass 2nd, 3rd, 4th, 5th st over the first st on RH needle.

(multiple of 9 sts plus 6)

Rows 1 and 5 (RS) *K2, p2, k2, p3; rep from *, end k2, p2, k2.

Rows 2, 4 and 6 K the knit sts and p the purl sts.

Row 3 *K2, p2, k2, p1, MB, p1; rep from *, end k2, p2, k2.

Rep rows 1–6.

23

M1P Make 1 st purlwise.

(worked over 20 sts)

Row 1 K2, p4, k2tog, k1, M1P, k2, M1P, k1, ssk, p4, k2.

Row 2 P2, k4, p2, k1, p2, k1, p2, k4, p2.

Row 3 K2, p3, k2tog, k1, p1, M1, k2, M1, p1, k1, ssk, p3, k2.

Row 4 P2, k3, p2, k1, p4, k1, p2, k3, p2.

Row 5 K2, p2, k2tog, k1, p1, k1, M1P, k2 M1P, k1, p1, k1, ssk, p2, k2.

Row 6 P2, k2, p2, k1, p1, k1, p2, k1, p1, k1, p2, k2, p2.

Row 7 K2, p1, k2tog, [k1, p1] twice, M1, k2, M1, [p1, k1] twice, ssk, p1, k2.

Row 8 P2, k1, p2, k1, p1, k1, p4, k1, p1, k1, p2, k1, p2.

Row 9 K2, k2tog, [k1, p1] twice, k1, M1P, k2, M1p, [k1, p1] twice, k1, ssk, k2.

Row 10 P4, [k1, p1] twice, k1, p2, [k1, p1] twice, k1, p4.

Row 11 K1, k2tog, [k1, p1] 3 times, M1, k2, M1, p1, [k1, p1] twice, k1, ssk, k1.

Row 12 P3, [k1, p1] twice, k1, p4, [k1, p1] twice, k1, p3.

Row 13 K2tog, [k1, p1] 3 times, k1, M1P, k2, M1P, [k1, p1] 3 times, k1, ssk.

Row 14 P2, [k1, p1] 3 times, k1, p2, [k1, p1] 3 times, k1, p2.

texture

25 on the edge

(worked over any number of sts)
Row 1 (WS) Knit.
Row 2 Knit.
Row 3 Purl.
Rep rows 2 and 3.

26 seed stitch

(worked over an odd number of sts)
Row 1 (RS) K1, *p1, k1; rep from * to end.
Row 2 K the purl sts and p the knit sts.
Rep row 2.

25

26

27 double moss stitch

(multiple of 4 sts)
Row 1 (RS) *K2, p2; rep from * to end.
Rows 2 and 4 K the knit sts and p the purl sts.
Row 3 *P2, k2; rep from * to end.
Rep rows 1–4.

28 picot de gallo

Pick up and k evenly around lower edge.
Purl 1 row.
Bind off 2 sts, *sl rem st from RH to LH needle, cast on 2 sts,
bind off 4 sts; rep from *, fasten off rem st.

texture

27

28

29 cast on, cast off

Picot Cast-On
Using cable cast-on method, *cast on 6 sts, bind off 2 sts, sl rem st from RH to LH needle; rep from * until 2 sts rem to be cast on, cast on 2 sts.

Picot Bind-Off
Bind off 4 sts, *sl rem st from RH to LH needle, cast on 2 sts, bind off 6 sts; rep from *, bind off final st.

30 double picot

Picot Cast-On
Using cable cast-on method, *cast on 4 sts, bind off 2 sts, sl rem st from RH to LH needle; rep from * until 2 sts rem to be cast on, cast on 2 sts.
K 6 rows.

Picot Bind-off
K 6 rows, then bind off as foll:
*Cast on 2 sts, bind off 4 sts. Place st from RH needle to LH needle; rep from * to end.

29

30

31 increasing ruffle

(worked over any number of sts)
Work 12 rows in St st.
Next (inc) row K into the front and back of each st.
Work 12 rows more in St st.
Bind off.

32 decreasing ruffle

(worked over an even number of sts)
Casts on twice as many sts as needed.
Work in St st for 2½"/6.5cm.
Next row *P2tog; rep from * to end.

31

32

33 pleated ruffle

(multiple of 10 sts plus 2)

Row 1 (RS) K4, *p4, k6; rep from *, end last rep k4.

Row 2 P4, *k4, p6; rep from *, end last rep p4.

Rows 3 and 5 Rep row 1.

Rows 4 and 6 Rep row 2.

Row 7 K2, *sl next 2 (knit) sts to cn and hold to *front*, sl next 4 (purl) sts to RH needle, sl next 2 (knit) sts to end of cn and hold to *front*, sl the 4 (purl) sts back to LH needle and [k1, st from cn at front with 1 st from LH needle at back tog] 4 times, k2; rep from *, end k2.

Row 8 K3, *k2tog, k4; rep from *, end k3.

Row 9 Knit.

34 tiny ruffles

DVD (double vertical decrease) Sl next 2 sts tog knitwise to RH needle, k1, pass 2 sl sts over k1.

(beg as a multiple of 7 plus 2, end as a multiple of 3 st plus 2)

Row 1 (WS) *K2, p5; rep from *, end k2.

Row 2 *P2, k1, DVD, k1; rep from *, end p2.

Row 3 *K2, p3; rep from *, end k2.

Row 4 *P2, DVD; rep from *, end p2.

Row 5 *K2, p1; rep from *, end k2.

Row 6 Knit.

33

34

35 raspberry ripple

(beg as a multiple of 10 sts plus 1, end as a multiple of 4 sts plus 1)

Row 1 (WS) K2, *p7, k3; rep from *, end last rep k2.

Row 2 P2, *k7, p3; rep from *, end last rep p2.

Row 3 Rep row 1.

Row 4 P2, *k2, sl 2, k1, p2sso, k2, p3; rep from *, end last rep p2.

Row 5 K2, *p5, k3; rep from *, end last rep k2.

Row 6 P2, *k1, sl 2, k1, p2sso, k1, p3; rep from *, end last rep p2.

Row 7 K2, *p3, k3; rep from *, end last rep k2.

Row 8 P2, *sl 2, k1, p2sso, p3; rep from *, end last rep p2.

Row 9 K2, *p1, k3; rep from *, end last rep k2.

36 bell ruffles

(multiple of 12 sts plus 3)

Row 1 (WS) K3, *p9, k3; rep from * to end.

Row 2 P3, *ssk, k5, k2tog, p3; rep from * to end.

Row 3 K3, *p7, k3; rep from * to end.

Row 4 P3, *ssk, k3, k2tog, p3; rep from * to end.

Row 5 K3, *p5, k3; rep from * to end.

Row 6 P3, *ssk, k1, k2tog, p3; rep from * to end.

Row 7 K3, *p3, k3; rep from * to end.

Row 8 P3, *S2KP, p3; rep from * to end.

Rows 9 to 11 K the knit sts and p the purl sts.

35

36

37 chevrons

(multiple of 20 sts plus 1)

Row 1 (RS) K1, *M1, k8, SK2P, k8, M1, k1; rep from * to end.

Rows 2, 3 and 4 Knit.

Rep rows 1–4.

38 lacy scallops

(multiple of 10 sts plus 1)

Rows 1, 2 and 3 Purl.

Rows 4, 6, 8, 10 and 12 (RS) *K1, yo, k3, SK2P, k3, yo; rep from *, end k1.

Rows 5, 7, 9, 11 and 13 Purl.

Row 14 Purl.

Rep rows 1–14.

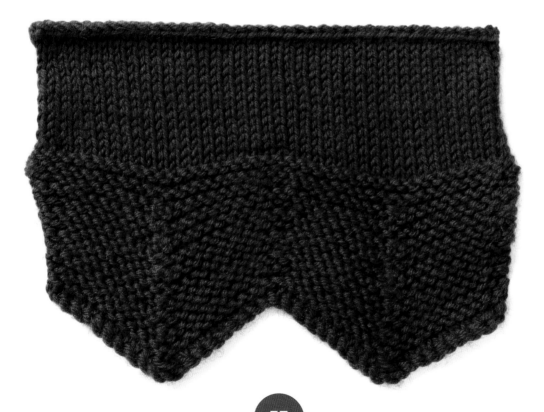

37

38

39 this way and that

(multiple of 5 sts plus 2)
Row 1 (RS) K1, *k1, p3, k1; rep from *, end k1.
Row 2 K1, *k3, p2; rep from *, end k1.
Row 3 K1, *p1, k2, p2; rep from *, end k1.
Row 4 K1, *k1, p2, k2; rep from *, end k1.
Row 5 K1, *p3, k2; rep from *, end k1.
Row 6 K1, *p1, k3, p1; rep from *, end k1.
Row 7 K1, *p3, k2; rep from *, end k1.
Row 8 K1, *k1, p2, k2; rep from *, end k1.
Row 9 K1, *p1, k2, p2; rep from *, end k1.
Row 10 K1, *k3, p2; rep from *, end k1.
Row 11 K1, *k1, p3, k1; rep from *, end k1.
Row 12 K1, *p2, k3; rep from *, end k1.
Rep rows 1–12.

40 textured triangles

(multiple of 10 sts plus 6)
Row 1 (RS)*K8, p2; rep from *, end k6.
Row 2 P5, k1, *k2, p7, k1; rep from * to end.
Row 3 *P2, k6, p2; rep from *, end p2, k4.
Row 4 P3, k3, *k2, p5, k3; rep from * to end.
Row 5 *P4, k4, p2; rep from *, end p4, k2.
Row 6 P1, k5, *k2, p3, k5; rep from * to end.
Row 7 *P6, k2, p2; rep from *, end p6.
Row 8 Rep row 6.
Row 9 Rep row 5.
Row 10 Rep row 4.
Row 11 Rep row 3.
Row 12 Rep row 2. Rep rows 1–12.

texture

39

40

41 granite relief stitch

(multiple of 2 sts)

Row 1 (RS) Knit.

Row 2 K2tog across.

Row 3 K into the front and back of each st.

Row 4 Purl.

Rep row 1–4.

42 bamboo stitch

(multiple of 2 sts)

Row 1 (RS) Sl 1, *yo to M1, k2, pass the M1 over the k2; rep from *, end k1.

Row 2 Sl 1, purl to the end.

Rep rows 1 and 2.

41

42

43 wispy twists

LT Knit the 2nd st tbl, then knit the first st tbl, then drop both sts from LH needle.

RT (worked on the WS) Purl 2nd st, then purl the first st, then drop both sts from LH needle.

(multiple of 4 sts plus 2)

Rows 1, 3 and 5 (RS) P1, *LT, p2; rep from *, end p1.

Rows 2 and 4 K1, *k2, RT; rep from *, end k1.

Row 6 K1, purl to last st, end k1.

Rows 7, 9 and 11 P1, *p2, LT; rep from *, end p1.

Rows 8 and 10 K1, *RT, k2; rep from *, end k1.

Row 12 Rep row 6.

Rep rows 1–12.

43

44 zigzags

RT With tip of RH needle, sl yo off LH needle knitwise, k next st, pass yo over k st.
LT Drop yo off LH needle and let it fall to back of work, insert RH needle between first and 2nd sts on LH needle and draw yo through to front, k next st, pass yo over k st.
(multiple of 2 sts plus 1)
Rows 1 and 3 (WS) P2, k1, *yo, sl 1, k1; rep from *, end p2.
Row 2 K2, *p1, RT; rep from *, end p1, k2.
Row 4 K2, *p1, LT; rep from *, end p1, k2.
Rep rows 1–4.

45 herringbone

RT K2tog and leave on LH needle, insert RH needle between the 2 sts and k the first st again, sl both sts from needle tog.
LT With RH needle behind LH needle, skip first st and k 2nd st tbl, then insert RH needle in back of both sts and k2tog tbl.
(multiple of 2 sts)
Rows 1, 2 and 3 Knit.
Row 4 (WS) Purl.
Row 5 K1, *RT; rep from *, end k1.
Rows 6, 8 and 10 Purl.
Row 7 K2, *RT; rep from *, end k2.
Row 9 K1, LT; rep from *, end k1.
Row 11 K2, *LT; rep from *, end k2.
Rows 12, 13 and 14 Knit.

44

45

(worked over an odd number of sts)

Row 1 (WS) *P2tog and leave sts on needle, p first st again, drop both sts tog from LH needle; rep from *, end k1.

Row 2 *Sl 1 wyib, k1, with tip of LH needle raise up sl st slightly, pull RH needle through raised st as for a psso but do not drop raised st from LH needle, k1 tbl of raised st and drop from needle; rep from *, end k1.

Rep rows 1 and 2.

46

47 rippling waves

(beg as a multiple of 2 sts plus 1 and end as a multiple of 1 st plus 1)

Row 1 (RS) K1, *k2, with tip of LH needle, sl first st over 2nd st on RH needle, rep from * to end.

Row 2 P1, *p2tog; rep from * to end.

Rows 3 Knit.

Rows 4 Purl.

Pick up same number of sts as in ruffle along edge of piece and join as foll:

With WS tog, *k 1 st from ruffle tog with 1 st from edge piece; rep from * to end.

48 double ruffle

First Ruffle

Pick up sts ½" above lower edge of piece.

K 1 row.

Inc row 1 K into front and back of each st.

Work in seed st for 5 rows.

Inc row 2 K into front and back of each st.

Work in seed st for 1 row.

Bind off in seed sts.

Second Ruffle

Pick up sts below first ruffle (¼" above lower edge of piece).

Work as for first ruffle.

47

48

(beg as a multiple of 2 sts plus 1 and end as a multiple of 1 st plus 1)

Lower Ruffle

Row 1 (RS) K1, *k2, with tip of LH needle, sl first st over 2nd st on RH needle, rep from * to end.

Row 2 P1, *p2tog; rep from * to end.

Rows 3, 5 and 7 Knit.

Rows 4, 6 and 8 Purl.

Place sts on spare needle.

Upper Ruffle

Work as for lower ruffle through row 4 only.

Join Ruffles

Next row (RS) Holding the 2 ruffles top, with top ruffle over lower ruffle, with MC, *k 1 st from lower ruffle with 1 st from top ruffle; rep from * across.

Purl 1 row.

50 to the point

*Cast on 2 sts.
Row 1 K2,
Rows 2–11 Yo, k to end—12 sts.
Leave on needle.
Rep from * for desired number of garter stitch points.

51 tabs and tassels

Cast on 3 sts.
*K 2 rows.
Row 3 (RS) Inc,1, k1, inc 1—5 sts.
Row 4 Knit.
Row 5 Inc 1, k to last st, inc 1—7 sts.
Rep rows 4 and 5 twice more—11 sts.
Leave sts on needle and cast on 3 sts.
Rep from * for each garter tab.

Make tassel for each tab as foll:
Wrap yarn around a piece of cardboard that is the
desired length of the tassel. Thread a strand of yarn,
insert it through the cardboard and tie it at the top,
leaving a long end to wrap around tassel.
Cut the lower edge to free the wrapped strands.
Wrap one long end of the yarn around the upper
edge and insert the yarn into the top. Trim the strands.

50

51

52 garter tabs

*Cast on 13 sts.

Work in St st for 14 rows.

Next row (RS) Knit, casting on 4 sts at end of row.

Slip to spare needle.*

Rep between *'s (as many times as desired number of tabs)

but cast on 14 sts.

Joining row Purl across all sts.

52

53 big bobbles

(multiple of 6 sts plus 2)

Row 1 (RS) P2, *k in front, back, front and back of next st (4 sts made in one st), p2, k1, p2; rep from * to end.

Rows 2 and 4 *K2, p1, k2, [k next st wrapping yarn twice around needle] 4 times; rep from *, end k2.

Rows 3 and 5 P2, *[k next st dropping extra yo] 4 times, p2, k1, p2; rep from * to end.

Row 6 *K2, p1, k2, p4tog; rep from *, end k2.

Row 7 P2, *k1, p2, k in front, back, front and back of next st (4 sts made in one st), p2; rep from * to end.

Rows 8 and 10 *K2, [k next st wrapping yarn twice around needle] 4 times, k2, p1; rep from *, end k2.

Rows 9 and 11 P2, *k1, p2, [k next st dropping extra yo] 4 times, p2; rep from * to end.

Row 12 *K2, p4tog, k2, p1; rep from * end k2.

Rep rows 1–12.

54 buoy bells

(beg as a multiple of 6 sts, end as a multiple of 7 sts plus 6)

Row 1 (RS) Purl.

Row 2 Knit.

Row 3 P6, *cast on 8 sts, p6; rep from * to end.

Rows 4 and 6 K6, *p8, k6; rep from * to end.

Row 5 P6, *k8, p6; rep from * to end.

Row 7 P6, *ssk, k4, k2tog, p6; rep from * to end.

Row 8 K6, *p6, k6; rep from * to end.

Row 9 P6, *ssk, k2, k2tog, p6; rep from * to end.

Row 10 K6, *p4, k6; rep from * to end.

Row 11 P6, *ssk, k2tog, p6; rep from * to end.

Row 12 K6, *p2, k6; rep from * to end.

Row 13 P6, *k2tog, p6; rep from * to end.

Row 14 K6, *p1 tbl, k6; rep from * to end.

Row 15 P6, *k1 tbl, p6; rep from * to end.

Rep rows 14 and 15 until desired length.

53

54

cables

55 simple twist

6-st RC Sl 3 sts to cn and hold to *back*, k3, k3 from cn.

(multiple of 11 sts plus 5)

Rows 1 and 3 (RS) Knit.

Rows 2, 4 and 6 *K5, p6; rep from *, end k5.

Row 5 K5, *6-st RC, k5; rep from * to end.

Rep rows 1–6.

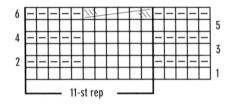

Stitch Key

☐ K on RS, p on WS

☐ P on RS, k on WS

▨ 6-st RC

56 cables and ribs

4-st RC Sl 2 sts to cn and hold to *back*, k2, k2 from cn.

4-st LC Sl 2 sts to cn and hold to *front*, k2, k2 from cn.

(multiple of 16 sts)

Row 1 (RS) *4-st LC, p3, k2, p3, 4-st RC; rep from * to end.

Row 2 and all WS rows *P4, k3, p2, k3, p4; rep from * to end.

Rows 3 and 5 *K4, p3, k2, p3, k4; rep from * to end.

Rep rows 1–6.

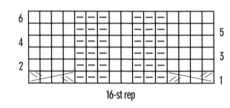

Stitch Key

☐ K on RS, p on WS

☐ P on RS, k on WS

▨ 4-st RC

▨ 4-st LC

57 slip 'n slide

12-st LC Sl 6 sts to cn and hold to *front,* k6, k6 from cn.

(multiple of 23 sts)

Rows 1, 3, 5, 9, 11, 13 and 15 (RS) Knit.

Row 2 and all WS rows *K3, p5, k3, p12; rep from * to end.

Row 7 *12-st LC, k11; rep from * to end.

Row 16 Rep row 2.

Rep rows 1–16.

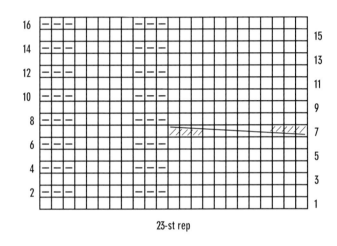

23-st rep

Stitch Key

☐ K on RS, p on WS

⊟ P on RS, k on WS

12-st LC

58 cables and columns

4-st LC Sl s sts to cn and hold to *front*, k2, p2 from cn.

(multiple of 10 sts)

Rows 1 and 5 (RS) *P1, k4, p1, k4, rep from * to end.

Rows 2 and 4 *P1, k2, p1, k1, p4, k1; rep from * to end.

Row 3 *P1, 4-st LC, p1, k4, rep from * to end.

Row 6 *P1, k2, p1, k1, p4, k1; rep from * to end.

Rep rows 1–6.

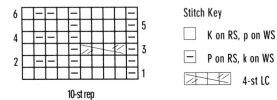

Stitch Key

☐ K on RS, p on WS

▬ P on RS, k on WS

⬚ 4-st LC

10-st rep

59 soft serve

6-st RC Sl 3 sts to cn and hold to *back*, k3, k3 from cn.

(multiple of 16 sts plus 10)

Rows 1 and 3 P2, k2, p2, *k6, p2, [k2, p2] twice; rep from *, end k2, p2.

Rows 2 and 4 K the knit sts and p the purl sts.

Row 5 P2, k2, p2, *6-st RC, p2, [k2, p2] twice; rep from *, end k2, p2.

Row 6 Rep row 2.

Rep rows 1–6 three times more.

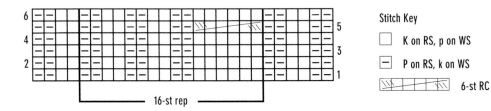

Stitch Key

☐ K on RS, p on WS

▬ P on RS, k on WS

⬚ 6-st RC

16-st rep

58

59

60 winding staircase

4-st RC Sl 2 sts to cn and hold to *back*, k2, k2 from cn.

(multiple of 18 sts)

Rows 1 and 5 (RS) *K1, p2, k2, p2, k4, p2, k2, p2, k1; rep from * to end.

Row 2 and all WS rows *P1, k2, p2, k2, p4, k2, p2, k2, p1; rep from * to end.

Row 3 *K1, p2, k2, p2, 4-st RC, p2, k2, p2, k1; rep from * to end.

Rep rows 1–6.

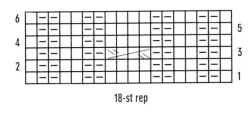

18-st rep

Stitch Key

☐ K on RS, p on WS

⊟ P on RS, k on WS

▧ 4-st RC

61 in a twist

4-st LC Sl 2 sts to cn and hold to *front*, k2, k2 from cn.

(multiple of 8 sts plus 6)

Row 1 (RS) P1, *k4, p4; rep from *, end k4, p1.

Row 2 and 4 K the knit sts and p the purl sts.

Row 3 P1, *4-st LC, p4; rep from *, end 4-st LC, p1.

Rep rows 1–4.

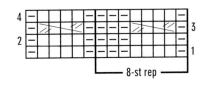

8-st rep

Stitch Key

☐ K on RS, p on WS

⊟ P on RS, k on WS

▧ 4-st LC

cables

62 garden rows

4-st LC Sl 2 sts to cn and hold to *front*, k2, k2 from cn.

(multiple of 7 sts plus 1)

Rows 1, 3 and 5 (WS) P1, k1, p4, k1, *p1 tbl, k1, p4, k1; rep from *, end p1.

Row 2 K1, *P1, 4-st LC, p1, k1 tbl; rep from *, end last rep k1.

Row 4 K1, *p1, k4, p1, k1 tbl; rep from *, end last rep k1.

Rep rows 2–5 six times more.

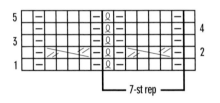

Stitch Key

☐ K on RS, p on WS

— P on RS, k on WS

Ω K1 tbl on RS, p1 tbl on WS

⧄ 4-st LC

62

63 back to back

4-st RC Sl 2 sts to cn and hold to *back*, k2, p2 from cn.

4-st LC Sl 2 sts to cn and hold to *front*, p2, k2 from cn.

(multiple of 30 sts)

Rows 1 and 5 (RS) *P2, [k2, p2] twice, k4, p1, k4, [p2, k2] twice, p2, k1; rep from * to end.

Row 2 and all WS rows *P1, k2, [k2, p2] twice, p4, k1, p4, [k2, p2] twice, k2; rep from * to end.

Rows 3 and 7 *P2, [k2, p2] twice, 4-st LC, p1, 4-st RC, [p2, k2] twice, p2, k1; rep from * to end.

Rep rows 1–8.

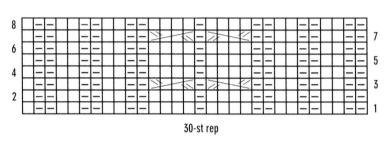

30-st rep

Stitch Key

☐ K on RS, p on WS

— P on RS, k on WS

⧄ 4-st RC

⧄ 4-st LC

63

64 corinthian columns

3-st LPC Sl 2 sts to cn and hold to *front*, k1; sl 1 st from cn to LH needle and p it; k1 from cn.

(multiple of 5 sts)

Rows 1, 3, 5, 7, 9, 11, 13, 15, 17, 19, 21, 23 and 27 *P2, k1 tbl, p1, k1 tbl; rep from * to end.

Rows 2, 4, 6, 8, 10, 12, 14, 16, 18, 20, 22, 24, 26 and 28 *P1 tbl, k1, p1 tbl, k2; rep from * to end.

Rows 25 and 29 *P2, 3-st LPC; rep from * to end.

Rows 30 and 32 *P3, k2; rep from * to end.

Row 31 *P2, k3; rep from * to end.

Row 33 *P3, k1, p1; rep from * to end.

Row 34 *K1, p1, k3; rep from * to end.

Rows 35, 37, 39, 41, 43 and 45 Purl.

Rows 36, 38, 40, 42, 44 and 46 Knit.

5-st rep

Stitch Key

☐ K on RS, p on WS

⊟ P on RS, k on WS

Ⓠ K1 tbl on RS, p1 tbl on WS

▷◁ 3-st LPC

65 hourglasses

6-st LPC Sl 2 sts to cn and hold to *front*, k2, p2, then k2 from cn.

(multiple of 8 sts plus 6)

Rows 1 and 5 (RS) K2, *p2, k2; rep from * to end.

Rows 2 and 6 P2, *k2, p2; rep from to end.

Row 3 K2, *p1, yo, 6-st LPC; rep from *, end p1, yo, p1, k2.

Row 4 P2, k2tog, k1, *p2, k2, p2, k2tog, k1; rep from *, end p2.

Rep rows 1–6.

cables

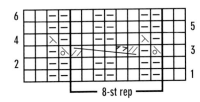

8-st rep

Stitch Key

☐ K on RS, p on WS

⊟ P on RS, k on WS

⊠ K2tog on RS, p2tog on WS

⧄ P1, yo

▱ 6-st LPC

66 solitary twist

8-st LC Sl 5 sts to cn and hold to *front*, k3, sl last 2 p sts from cn to LH needle, move cn to back, p2, k3 from cn.

(multiple of 26 sts plus 14)

Rows 1, 3 and 5 (RS) *K3, p3, k2, p3, [k3, p2] 3 times; rep from *, end, k3, p3, k2, p3, k3.

Row 2 and all WS rows P3, k3, p2, k3, p3, *[k2, p3] 3 times, k3, p2, k3, p3; rep from * to end.

Row 7 *K3, p3, k2, p3, k3, p2, 8-st LC, p2; rep from *, end k3, p3, k2, p3, k3.

Rep rows 1–8.

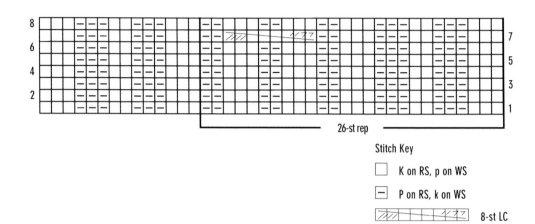

26-st rep

Stitch Key

☐ K on RS, p on WS

— P on RS, k on WS

8-st LC

67 double twist

LT
Row 1 (RS) Skip first st on LH needle and k 2nd st behind the first st, then k first st and drop both sts from LH needle.
Row 2 P2.
Rep rows 1 and 2 for LT.

6-st LC
Rows 1 and 3 (RS) K6.
Rows 2, 4 and 6 P6.
Row 5 Sl 3 sts to cn and hold to *front*, k3, k3 from cn.
Rep rows 1–6 for 6-st LC.

8-st RC
Rows 1, 3, 5 and 7 (RS) K8.
Rows 2, 4, 6, 8 and 10 P8.
Row 9 Sl 4 sts to cn and hold to *back*, k4, k4 from cn.
Rep rows 1–10 for 8-st RC.

(worked over 30 sts)
Row 1 (RS) P2, LT, p2, 8-st RC, p2, k3, p2, 6-st LC, p3.
Cont in pats as established, working sts outside cable pats as you k the knit sts and p the purl sts.

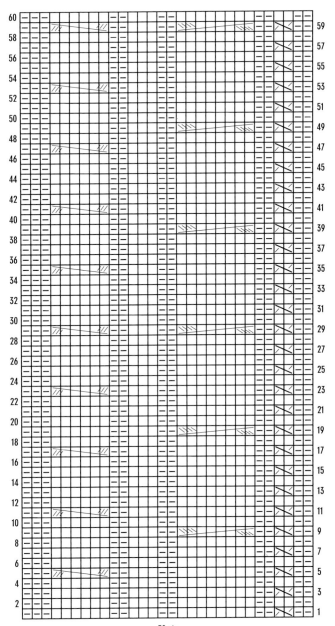

30 sts

Stitch Key

☐ K on RS, p on WS

⊟ P on RS, k on WS

⧄ LT

▱ 6-st LC

▱ 8-st RC

67

68 tug of war

6-st LC Sl 3 sts to cn and hold to *front*, k3, k3 from cn.

(worked over 16 sts)

Note Sts for St st were picked up after edging was knit.

Rows 1 and 5 (RS) K1, p4, k6, p4, k1.

Rows 2, 4 and 6 K5, p6, k5.

Row 3 K1, p4, sl 6-st LC, p4, k1.

Rep rows 1–6.

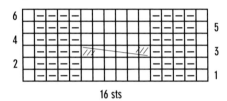

16 sts

Stitch Key

☐ K on RS, p on WS

⊟ P on RS, k on WS

▨ 6-st LC

68

69 taffy pull

10-st LC Sl 5 sts to cn and hold to *front*, k5, k5 from cn.

(worked over 10 sts)

Note Sts for St st were picked up after edging was knit.

Rows 1, 3, 5 and 7 (WS) Purl.

Rows 2, 4 and 8 Knit.

Row 6 Sl 5 sts to cn and hold to *front*, k5, k5 from cn.

Rows 1–8.

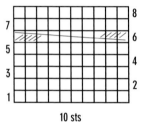

10 sts

Stitch Key

☐ K on RS, p on WS

⊟ P on RS, k on WS

▨ 10-st LC

69

6-st RC Sl 3 sts to cn and hold to *back*, k3, k3 from cn. (over 16 sts)

Note Sts for St st were picked up after edging was knit.

Row 1 (RS) P2, [6-st RC] twice, p2.

Rows 2, 4 and 6 K2, p12, k2.

Row 3 P2, k2, 6-st RC, k4, p2.

Rows 5 and 7 P2, k12, p2.

Row 8 K2, p12, k2.

Rep rows 1–8 until desired length.

Bind off 16 sts, leaving last st. With RS facing, pick up and knit evenly along side edge. Work as desired.

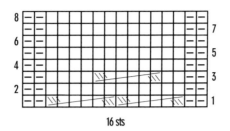

16 sts

Stitch Key

☐ K on RS, p on WS

⊟ P on RS, k on WS

▨ 6-st RC

70

71 rope-a-dope

8-st RC Sl 4 sts to cn and hold to *back*, k4, k4 from cn.
(worked over 12 sts)
Note Sts for St st were picked up after edging was knit.
Rows 1 and 3 (RS) P2, k8, p2.
Rows 2, 4 and 6 K2, p8, k2.
Row 5 P2, 8-st RC, p2.
Rep rows 1–6.

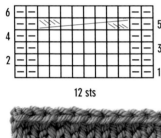

12 sts

Stitch Key

☐ K on RS, p on WS

▬ P on RS, k on WS

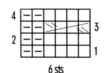 8-st RC

72 twisted trim

4-st RC Sl 2 sts to cn and hold to *back*, k2, k2 from cn.
(worked over 6 sts)
Note Sts for St st were picked up after edging was knit.
Row 1 (RS) K4, p2.
Row 2 K2, p4.
Row 3 4-st RC, p2.
Row 4 K2, p4.
Rep rows 1–4.

6 sts

Stitch Key

☐ K on RS, p on WS

▬ P on RS, k on WS

4-st RC

71

72

73 grecian formula

3-st RC Sl 2 sts to cn and hold to *back*, k1, k2 from cn.

6-st RC Sl 3 sts to cn and hold to *back*, k3, k3 from cn.

Chart 1

(worked over 12 sts)

Rows 1, 3 and 5 (WS) P1, k2, p6, k2, p1.

Rows 2 and 4 P1, k1, p1, k6, p1, k1, p1.

Row 6 P1, k1, p1, 6-st RC, p1, k1, p1.

Rep rows 1–6.

Chart 2

(multiple of 9 sts)

Rows 1 and 3 (WS) P1, k2, p3, k2, p1.

Row 2 K1, p2, 3-st RC, p2, k1.

Row 4 K1, p2, k3, p2, k1.

Rep rows 1–4.

Cast on 12 sts. Work rows 1–6 of chart 1 until desired length.

Bind off 11 sts, leaving last st. With RS facing, pick up and knit a multiple of 9 sts evenly along side edge. Work rows 1–4 of chart 2 until desired length.

Chart 1

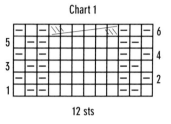

12 sts

Chart 2

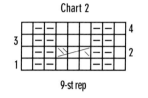

9-st rep

Stitch Key

☐ K on RS, p on WS

⊟ P on RS, k on WS

3-st RC

6-st RC

74 peek-a-boo bobbles

4-st RC Sl 2 sts to cn and hold to *back*, k2, k2 from cn.

4-st LC Sl 2 sts to cn and hold to *front*, k2, k2 from cn.

Make Bobble (MB) K in front, back and front of st, turn, p3, turn, SK2P.

(multiple of 14 sts plus 8)

Row 1 (RS) P2, *4-st RC, p1, MB, p1, 4-st LC, p1, MB, p1; rep from *,
end 4-st RC, p2.

Row 2 and all WS rows K2, p4, *k3, p4; rep from *, end k2.

Rows 3 and 5 P2, *k4, p3; rep from *, end k4, p2.

Rep rows 1–6.

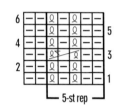

Stitch Key

☐ K on RS, p on WS

⊟ P on RS, k on WS

● MB

▨ 4-st RC

▨ 4-st LC

75 cablegrams

3-st RPC Sl 2 sts to cn and hold to *back*, k1 tbl, (p1, k1 tbl)
from cn.

(multiple of 5 sts plus 2)

Rows 1 and 5 (RS) *P2, k1 tbl, p1, k1 tbl; rep from * end p2.

Rows 2, 4 and 6 K2, *p1 tbl, k1, p1 tbl; rep from * end k2.

Row 3 *P2, RT; rep from * end p2.

Rep rows 1–6.

Stitch Key

☐ K on RS, p on WS

⊟ P on RS, k on WS

Ω K1 tbl on RS, p1 tbl on WS

▨ 3-st RPC

RT K2tog, do not sl off needle, k first st, sl both sts off needle.

LT K 2nd st tbl, do not sl off needle, k first st, sl both sts off needle.

(multiple of 19 sts plus 8)

Rows 1, 3 and 7 (RS) *P2, k4, p2, k2tog, k3, M1, k1, M1, k3, SKP; from *, end p2, k4, p2.

Rows 2, 4, 6 and 8 K2, p4, k2, *p11, k2, p4, k2; rep from * to end.

Row 5 *P2, RT, LT, p2, k2tog, k3, M1, k1, M1, k3, SKP; rep from *, end p2, RT, LT, p2.

Rep rows 1–8.

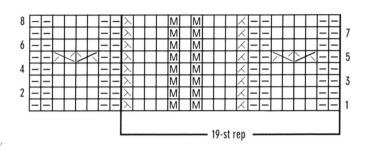

Stitch Key

☐ K on RS, p on WS

— P on RS, k on WS

Ⓜ M1

⧄ SKP

⧅ K2tog

⧄ RT

⧄ LT

77 climbing vines

2-st RPC Sl 1 st to cn and hold to *back*, k1 tbl, p1 from cn.

2-st LPC Sl 1 st to cn and hold to *front*, p1, k1 tbl from cn.

(multiple of 13 sts)

Row 1 (RS) K2, p3, k3 tbl, p3, k2.

Row 2 P2, k3, p3 tbl, k3, p2.

Row 3 K2, p2, 2-st RPC, k1 tbl, 2-st LPC, p2, k2.

Row 4 P2, k2, p1 tbl, k1, p1 tbl, k1, p1 tbl, k2, p2.

Row 5 K2, p1, 2-st RPC, p1, k1 tbl, p1, 2-st LPC, p1, k2.

Row 6 P2, k1, p1 tbl, k2, p1, k2, p1 tbl, k1, p2.

Row 7 K2, 2-st RPC, p1, k3 tbl, p1, 2-st LPC, k2.

Row 8 P2, p1 tbl, k2, p3 tbl, k2, p1 tbl, p2.

Rep rows 1–8.

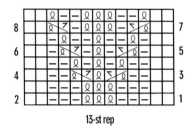

13-st rep

Stitch Key

☐ K on RS, p on WS

— P on RS, k on WS

Ⴓ K1 tbl on RS, p1 tbl on WS

2-st RPC

2-st LPC

78 espalier

cables

RPT Sl 1 st to cn and hold to *back*, k1, p1 from cn.

LPT Sl 1 st to cn and hold to *front*, p1, k1 from cn.

(multiple of 15 sts plus 4)

Row 1 (RS) *K4 tbl, p4, k3 tbl, p4; rep from *, end k4 tbl.

Row 2 P4 tbl, *k4, p3 tbl, k4, p4 tbl; rep from * to end.

Row 3 *K4 tbl, p3, RPT, k1 tbl, LPT, p3; rep from *, end k4tbl.

Row 4 P4 tbl, *k3, [p1 tbl, p1] twice, p1 tbl, k3, p4 tbl; rep from *
to end.

Row 5 *K4 tbl, p2, RPT, p1, k1 tbl, p1, LPT, p2; rep from *, end k4 tbl.

Row 6 P4 tbl, *[k2, p1 tbl] 3 times, k2, p4 tbl; rep from * to end.

Row 7 *K4 tbl, p1, RPT, p2, k1 tbl, p2, LPT, p1; rep from *, end k4 tbl.

Row 8 P4 tbl, *k1, p1 tbl, k3, p1 tbl, k3, p1 tbl, k1, p4 tbl; rep from *
to end.

Row 9 *K4 tbl, RPT, p3, k1 tbl, p3, LPT; rep from *, end k4 tbl.

Row 10 P4 tbl, *[p1 tbl, k4] twice, p5 tbl; rep from * to end.

Rep rows 1–10.

Stitch Key

Ⓠ K1 tbl on RS, p1 tbl on WS

▭ P on RS, k on WS

⧅ RPT

⧅ LPT

15-st rep

4-st RPC Sl 2 sts to cn and hold to *back*, k2, p2 from cn.

4-st LPC Sl 2 sts to cn and hold to *back*, p2, k2 from cn.

4-st RC Sl 2 sts to cn and hold to *back*, k2, k2 from cn.

4-st LC Sl 2 sts to cn and hold to *back*, k2, k2 from cn.

(multiple of 48 sts)

Row 1 *[P2, k2] 5 times, 4-st RC, p2, 4-st LC, [k2, p2] 4 times, k2; rep from * to end.

Row 2 *[P2, k2] 4 times, [p6, k2] twice, [p2, k2] 4 times; rep from * to end.

Row 3 *[P2, k2] 4 times, p2, 4-st RPC, k2, p2, k2, 4-st LPC, [p2, k2] 4 times; rep from * to end.

Rows 4, 8, 12, 16, 20, 24, 28 and 32 *P2, k2; rep from * to end.

Row 5 *[P2, k2] 4 times, 4-st RC, [p2, k2] twice, p2, 4-st LC, [k2, p2] 3 times, k2; rep from * to end.

Row 6 *[P2, k2] 3 times, p6, [k2, p2] twice, k2, p6, [k2, p2] 3 times, k2; rep from * to end.

Row 7 *[P2, k2] 3 times, p2, 4-st RPC, [k2, p2] 3 times, k2, 4-st LPC, [p2, k2] 3 times; rep from * to end.

Row 9 *[P2, k2] 3 times, 4-st RC, [p2, k2] 4 times, p2, 4-st LC, [k2, p2] twice, k2; rep from * to end.

Rows 10 and 22 *[P2, k2] twice, p6, [k2, p2] 4 times, k2, p6, [k2, p2] twice, k2; rep from * to end.

Row 11 *[P2, k2] twice, p2, 4-st RPC, [k2, p2] 5 times, k2, 4-st LPC, [p2, k2] twice; rep from * to end.

Row 13 *[P2, k2] twice, 4-st RC, [p2, k2] twice, 4-st RC, p2, 4-st LC, [k2, p2] twice, 4-st LC, k2, p2, k2; rep from * to end.

Row 14 *[P2, k2, p6, k2] twice, [p6, k2, p2, k2] twice; rep from * to end.

Row 15 *P2, k2, p2, 4-st RPC, [k2, p2] twice, 4-st RPC, k2, p2, k2, 4-st LPC, [p2, k2] twice, 4-st LPC, p2, k2; rep from * to end.

Row 17 *P2, k2, 4-st RC, [p2, k2] twice, 4-st RC, [p2, k2] twice, p2, 4-st LC, [k2, p2] twice, 4-st LC, k2; rep from * to end.

Row 18 *[P6, k2, p2, k2] twice, [p2, k2, p6, k2] twice; rep from * to end.

Row 19 *P2, 4-st RPC, [k2, p2] twice, 4-st RPC, [k2, p2] 3 times, k2, 4-st LPC, [p2, k2] twice, 4-st LPC; rep from * to end.

Row 21 *[P2, k2] 3 times, 4-st RC, [p2, k2] 4 times, p2, 4-st LC, [k2, p2] twice, k2; rep from * to end.

Row 23 *[P2, k2] twice, p2, 4-st RPC, [k2, p2] 5 times, k2, 4-st LPC, [p2, k2] twice; rep from * to end.

Row 25 *[P2, k2] twice, 4-st RC, [p2, k2] 6 times, p2, 4-st LC, k2, p2, k2; rep from * to end.

Row 26 *P2, k2, p6, k2, [p2, k2] 6 times, p6, k2, p2, k2; rep from * to end.

Row 27 *P2, k2, p2, 4-st RPC, [k2, p2] 7 times, k2, 4-st LPC, p2, k2; rep from * to end.

Row 29 *P2, k2, 4-st RC, [p2, k2] 8 times, p2, 4-st LC, k2; rep from * to end.

Row 30 *P6, k2, [p2, k2] 8 times, p6, k2; rep from * to end.

Row 31 *P2, 4-st RPC, [k2, p2] 9 times, k2, 4-st LPC; rep from * to end.

79

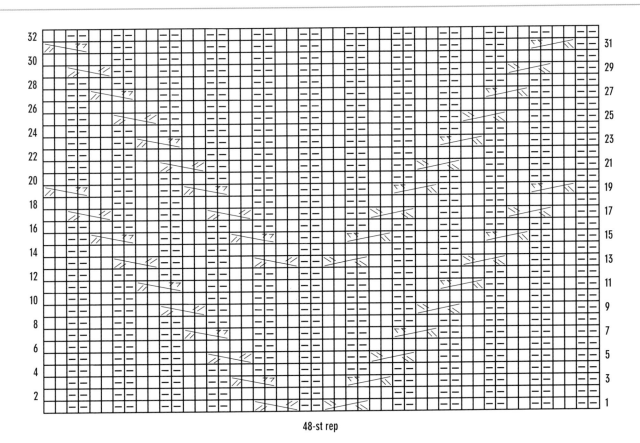

48-st rep

cables

Stitch Key

☐   K on RS, p on WS

—   P on RS, k on WS

⧅⧅   4-st RC

⧅⧅   4-st LC

⧅⧅   4-st RPC

⧅⧅   4-st LPC

3-st LC Sl 1 st to cn and hold to *front*, k2, k1 from cn.

3-st RPC Sl 1 st to cn and hold to *back*, k2, p1 from cn.

3-st LPC Sl 2 sts to cn and hold to *back*, p1, k2 from cn.

4-st RC Sl 2 sts to cn and hold to *back*, k2, k2 from cn.

4-st LC Sl 2 sts to cn and hold to *back*, k2, k2 from cn.

(over 40 sts)

Row 1 K1, p1, 3-st LC, p3, [3-st LPC, p2, 3-st RPC] twice, 3-st LPC, p2, 3-st RPC, p3, 3-st LC, p1, k1.

Row 2 K2, p3, k4, [p2, k2] 5 times, p2, k4, p3, k2.

Rows 3 and 11 K1, p1, k3, p4, 3-st LPC, 3-st RPC, p2, 3-st LPC, 3-st RPC, p2, 3-st LPC, 3-st RPC, p4, k3, p1, k1.

Rows 4 and 6 K2, p3, k5, [p4, k4] twice, p4, k5, p3, k2.

Rows 5 and 13 K1, p1, 3-st LC, p5, 4-st RC, [p4, 4-st RC] twice, p5, 3-st LC, p1, k1.

Rows 7 and 15 K1, p1, k3, p4, [3-st RPC, 3-st LPC, p2] twice, 3-st RPC, 3-st LPC, p4, k3, p1, k1.

Rows 8 and 10 K2, p3, k4, [p2, k2] 5 times, p2, k4, p3, k2.

Row 9 K1, p1, 3-st LC, p4, [k2, p2] 5 times, k2, p4, 3-st LC, p1, k1.

Rows 12 and 14 K2, p3, k5, [p4, k4] twice, p4, k5, p3, k2.

Row 16 K2, p3, k4, [p2, k2] 5 times, p2, k4, p3, k2.

Row 17 K1, p1, 3-st LC, p3, 3-st RPC, [p2, 3-st LPC, 3-st RPC] twice, p2, 3-st LPC, p3, 3-st LC, p1, k1.

Rows 18 and 28 K2, p3, k3, p2, [k4, p4] twice, k4, p2, k3, p3, k2.

Row 19 K1, p1, k3, p2, 3-st RPC, [p4, 4-st LC] twice, p4, 3-st LPC, p2, k3, p1, k1.

Rows 20 and 26 K2, p3, k2, p2, k5, p4, k4, p4, k5, p2, k2, p3, k2.

Row 21 K1, p1, 3-st LC, p1, 3-st RPC, p4, 3-st RPC, 3-st LPC, p2, 3-st RPC, 3-st LPC, p4, 3-st LPC, p1, 3-st LC, p1, k1.

Rows 22 and 24 K2, p3, k1, p2, k5, [p2, k2] 3 times, p2, k5, p2, k1, p3, k2.

Row 23 K1, p1, k3, p1, k2, p5, [k2, p2] 3 times, k2, p5, k2, p1, k3, p1, k1.

Row 25 K1, p1, 3-st LC, p1, 3-st LPC, p4, 3-st LPC, 3-st RPC, p2, 3-st LPC, 3-st RPC, p4, 3-st RPC, p1, 3-st LC, p1, k1.

Row 27 K1, p1, k3, p2, 3-st LPC, [p4, 4-st LC] twice, p4, 3-st RPC, p2, k3, p1, k1.

Stitch Key

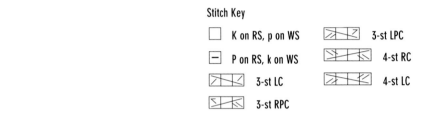

☐ K on RS, p on WS

☐ P on RS, k on WS

3-st LC

3-st RPC

3-st LPC

4-st RC

4-st LC

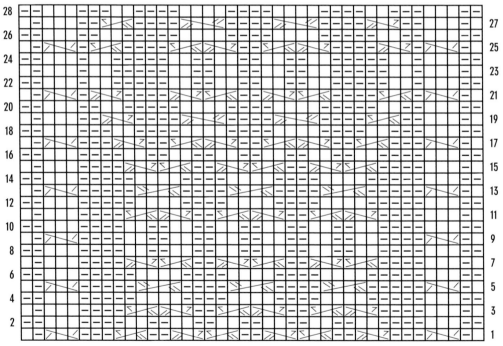

40 sts

81 cyclone

5-st RPC Sl 2 sts to cn and hold to *back*, k3, p2 from cn.
5-st LPC Sl 3 sts to cn and hold to *front*, p2, k3 from cn.
6-st RC Sl 3 sts to cn and hold to *back*, k3, k3 from cn.
6-st LC Sl 3 sts to cn and hold to *front*, k3, k3 from cn.
(worked over 26 sts)

Row 1 (RS) K1, p2, k3, p4, 6-st LC, p4, k3, p2, k1.

Rows 2, 4 and 14 K3, p3, k4, p6, k4, p3, k3.

Rows 3 and 15 K1, p2, k3, p4, k6, p4, k3, p2, k1.

Row 5 K1, p2, 5-st LPC, p2, k6, p2, 5-st RPC, p2, k1.

Rows 6 and 12 K5, p3, k2, p6, k2, p3, k5.

Row 7 K1, p4, 5-st LPC, 6-st LC, 5-st RPC, p4, k1.

Rows 8 and 10 K7, p12, k7.

Row 9 K1, p6, [6-st RC] twice, p6, k1.

Row 11 K1, p4, 5-st RPC, 6-st LC, 5-st LPC, p4, k1.

Row 13 K1, p2, 5-st RPC, p2, k6, p2, 5-st LPC, p2, k1.

Row 16 Rep row 2.

Rep rows 1–16.

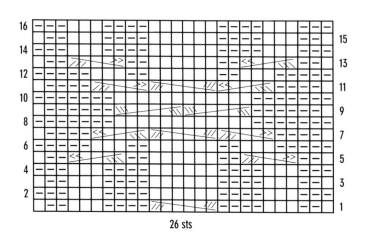

26 sts

Stitch Key

☐ K on RS, p on WS

⊟ P on RS, k on WS

▨ 5-st RPC

▨ 5-st LPC

▨ 6-st RC

▨ 6-st LC

81

3-st RPC Sl 1 st to cn and hold to *back*, k2, p1 from cn.
3-st LPC Sl 2 sts to cn and hold to *front*, p1, k2 from cn.
4-st RC Sl 2 sts to cn and hold to *back*, k2, k2 from cn.
4-st LC Sl 2 sts to cn and hold to *front*, k2, k2 from cn.
(worked over 30 sts)
Note Sts for St st were picked up after edging was knit.
Row 1 (RS) K1, [p4, 4-st RC] 3 times, p4, k1.
Row 2 K1, p1, k3, [p4, k4] twice, p4, k3, p1, k1.
Row 3 K1, p3, 3-st RPC, [4-st LC, 4-st RC] twice, 3-st LPC, p3, k1.

Row 4 K1, p1, k2, p2, k3, p4, k4, p4, k3, p2, k2, p1, k1.
Row 5 K1, p2, 3-st RPC, p3, 4-st LC, p4, 4-st RC, p3, 3-st LPC, p2, k1.
Row 6 K1, p1, k1, p2, [k4, p4] twice, k4, p2, k1, p1, k1.
Row 7 K1, p2, k2, p3, 3-st RPC, 4-st LC, 4-st RC, 3-st LPC, p3, k2, p2, k1.
Row 8 K1, p1, k1, [p2, k3] twice, p4, [k3, p2], k1, p1, k1.
Row 9 K1, p2, [k2, p3] twice, 4-st RC, [p3, k2] twice, p2, k1.
Row 10 Rep row 8.

Row 11 K1, p2, k2, p3, 3-st LPC, 4-st RC, 4-st LC, 3-st RPC, p3, k2, p2, k1.
Row 12 Rep row 6.
Row 13 K1, p2, 3-st LPC, p3, 4-st LC, p4, 4-st RC, p3, 3-st RPC, p2, k1.
Row 14 Rep row 4.
Row 15 K1, p3, 3-st LPC, [4-st RC, 4-st LC] twice, 3-st RPC, p3, k1.
Row 16 K1, p1, k3, [p4, k4] twice, p4, k3, p1, k1.

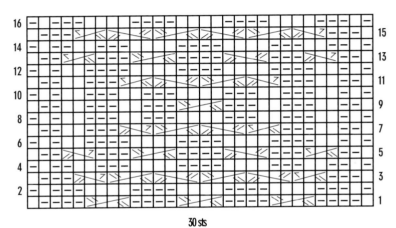

30 sts

Stitch Key
☐ K on RS, p on WS
⊟ P on RS, k on WS
3-st RPC
3-st LPC
4-st RC
4-st LC

83 twister

3-st RPC Sl 1 st to cn and hold to *back*, k2, p1 from cn.

3-st LPC Sl 2 sts to cn and hold to *front*, p1, k2 from cn.

4-st RC Sl 2 sts to cn and hold to *back*, k2, k2 from cn.

4-st LC Sl 2 sts to cn and hold to *front*, k2, k2 from cn.

4-st RPC Sl 2 sts to cn and hold to *back*, k2, p2 from cn.

4-st LPC Sl 2 sts to cn and hold to *front*, p2, k2 from cn.

Double inc K1, p1 and k1 into one st.

4-st dec On WS, drop yarn, sl 3 sts purlwise to RH needle, *pass 2nd st on RH needle over the first (center) st, sl center st back to LH needle and pass 2nd st on LH needle over it*, sl center st back to RH needle and rep between *'s once. Then, with dropped yarn, k1 into this st.

(panel of 28 sts increased to 32 sts)

Note Sl all sts purlwise with yarn in back.

Rows 1 and 3 (WS) P1, k9, p4, k5, p4, k4, p1.

Row 2 Sl 1, p4, 4-st RC, p5, 4-st RC, p9, sl 1.

Row 4 Sl 1, p3, [3-st RPC, 3-st LPC, p3] twice, M1, double inc, M1, p4, sl 1.

Row 5 P1, k4, p2, k1, p2, k3, p2, k2, p2, p3, k2, p2, k2, p3, k1.

Row 6 Sl 1, p2, 3-st RPC, p2, 4-st LPC, 3-st RPC, p2, 3-st LPC, 4-st RC, p1, 4-st LPC, p2, sl 1.

Rows 7 and 9 P1, k2, p2, k5, p4, k4, p4, k5, p2, k2, p1.

Row 8 Sl 1, p2, k2, p5, 4-st LC, p4, 4-st LC, p5, k2, p2, sl 1.

Row 10 Sl 1, p2, 4-st LPC, p1, 4-st RPC, 3-st LPC, p2, 3-st RPC, 4-st LPC, p2, 3-st RPC, p2 sl 1.

Row 11 P1, k3, p2, k2, p2, k3, p2, k2, p2, k3, 4-st decrease, k4, p1.

Row 12 Sl 1, p8, 3-st LPC, 3-st RPC, p3, 3-st LPC, 3-st RPC, p3, sl 1.

Row 13 P1, k4, p4, k5, p4, k9, p1.

Row 14 Sl 1, p9, 4-st RC, p5, 4-st RC, p4, sl 1.

Row 15 P1 k4, p4, k5, p5, k8, p1.

Row 16 Sl 1, p4, M1, double inc, M1, [p3, 3-st RPC, 3-st LPC] twice, p3, sl 1.

Row 17 P1, k3, p2, k2, p2, k3, p2, k2, p2, k3, p2, k1, k2, k4, p1.

Row 18 Sl 1, p2, 4-st RPC, p1, 4-st LPC, 3-st RPC, p2, 3-st LPC, 4-st RC, p2, 3-st LPC, p2, sl 1.

Rows 19 and 21 P1, k2, p2, k5, p4, k4, p4, k5, p2, k2, p1.

Row 20 Sl 1, p2, k2, p5, 4-st LC, p4, 4-st LC, p5, k2, p2, sl 1.

Row 22 Sl 1, p2, 3-st LPC, p2, 4-st RPC, 3-st LPC, p2, 3-st RPC, 4-st LPC, p1, 4-st RPC, p2, sl 1.

Row 23 P1, k4, 4-st decrease, k3, p2, k2, p2, k3, p2, k2, p2, k3, p1.

Row 24 Sl 1, [p3, 3-st LPC, 3-st RPC] twice, p8, sl 1.

Rep rows 1–24.

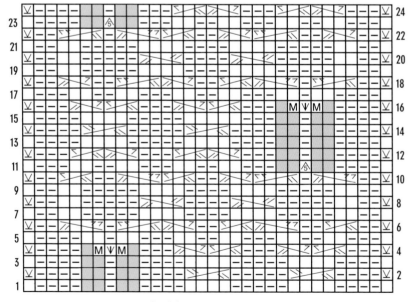

Panel of 28 sts increased to 32

Stitch Key

☐ K on RS, p on WS

▬ P on RS, k on WS

Ⓜ M1

Ⓥ Double inc

☑ Sl st purlwise wyib

Ⓐ 4-st decrease

⧑ 3-st RPC

⧑ 3-st LPC

⧑ 4-st RC

⧑ 4-st LC

⧑ 4-st RPC

⧑ 4-st LPC

▨ No stitch

lace

84 connect the dots

(worked over an odd number of sts)
Row 1 (RS) and 2 Purl.
Row 3 (RS) Knit.
Row 4 Purl.
Row 5 K2, *yo, p2tog; rep from *, end k1.
Row 6 Knit.
Row 7 Knit.

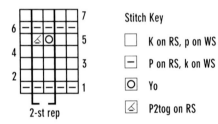

2-st rep

Stitch Key

☐ K on RS, p on WS

⊟ P on RS, k on WS

☉ Yo

⟋ P2tog on RS

85 caterpillars

(multiple of 4 plus 3)
Row 1 (WS) P2, *k1, yo, k2tog, p1; rep from, end p1.
Row 2 K2, *p1, k1; rep from *, end k1.
Rows 3–6 Rep rows 1 and 2 twice more.

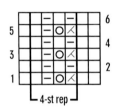

4-st rep

Stitch Key

☐ K on RS, p on WS

⊟ P on RS, k on WS

☉ Yo

⟋ K2tog

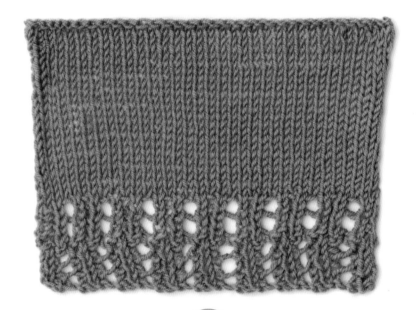

86 honeycomb stripes

(multiple of 4 sts plus 2)
Row 1 (RS) K1, *ssk, yo, p1, k1; rep from *, end k.
Row 2 K1, *p2tog, yo, k1, p1; rep from *, end k1.
Rep rows 1 and 2.

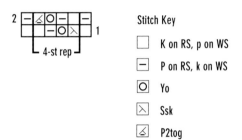

Stitch Key

☐ K on RS, p on WS

⊟ P on RS, k on WS

⊡ Yo

⊠ Ssk

◹ P2tog

87 tracks

(multiple of 6 sts plus 2)
Row 1 (WS) *P2, k1; rep from *, end p2.
Row 2 *K2, p1, yo, ssk, p1; rep from *, end k2.
Row 3 Rep row 1.
Row 4 *K2, p1, k2tog, yo, p1; rep from *, end k2.
Rep rows 1–4.

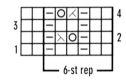

Stitch Key

☐ K on RS, p on WS

⊟ P on RS, k on WS

⊠ SKP

◺ K2tog

⊡ Yo

lace

86

87

88 millipedes

S2KP Sl 2 sts tog as if to k2tog, k1, pass the 2 sl sts over the k1.

(multiple of 6 plus 1)

Row 1 (RS) K1, *yo, k1, S2KP, k1, yo, k1; rep from * to end.

Row 2 Purl.

Rep rows 1 and 2.

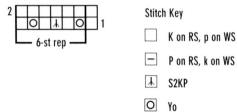

Stitch Key

☐ K on RS, p on WS

⊟ P on RS, k on WS

⊼ S2KP

⊙ Yo

89 sidewalk scene

(multiple of 16 sts plus 6)

Rows 1, 3, 5, 7 and 9 (WS) K1, *k5, p3, k4, p4; rep from *, k5.

Rows 2 and 6 P5, *yo, k2tog, ssk, yo, p4, yo, ssk, k1, p5; rep from *, end p1.

Rows 4 and 8 P5, *yo, k2tog, ssk, yo, p4, k1, yo, ssk, p5; rep from *, end p1.

Rows 10 and 11 Purl.

Row 12 K5, *[yo, k2tog, ssk, yo, k4] twice; rep from *, end k1.

Row 13 Knit.

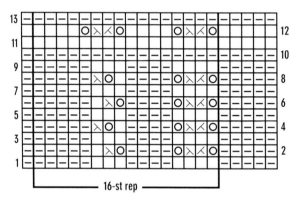

Stitch Key

☐ K on RS, p on WS

⊟ P on RS, k on WS

⊠ Ssk

⧅ K2tog

⊙ Yo

90 crescent moons

S2KP Sl 2 sts tog as if to k2tog, k1, pass the 2 sl sts over the k1.
(multiple of 8 sts)
Row 1 (RS) K4, *yo, S2KP, yo, k5; rep from *, end yo, S2KP, yo, k1.
Rows 2, 4 and 6 Purl.

Row 3 *K3, yo, k1, S2KP, k1, yo; rep from * to end.
Row 5 K2, *yo, k2, S2KP, k2, yo, k1; rep from *, end yo, k2, S2KP, k1, yo.
Row 7 Knit.

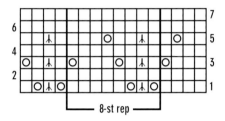

Stitch Key

☐ K on RS, p on WS

― P on RS, k on WS

⋏ S2KP

Ⓞ Yo

91 eyelets and scallops

(multiple of 8 sts plus 3)
Row 1 (RS) K2, *yo, k2, SK2P, k2, yo, k1; rep from * to last st, k1.
Row 2 Purl.
Rep rows 1 and 2.

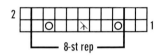

Stitch Key

☐ K on RS, p on WS

Ⓞ Yo

⋏ SK2P

lace

92 argyle

(multiple of 10 plus 3)

Row 1 (RS) K1, *k1, yo, k3, SK2P, k3, yo; rep from *, end k2.

Rows 2, 4 and 6 Purl.

Row 3 K1, *k2, yo, k2, SK2P, k2, yo, k1; rep from *, end k2.

Row 5 K1, k2tog, *[yo, k1] twice, SK2P, [k1, yo] twice, SK2P; rep from *, end yo, k1, yo, k1, SK2P, [k1, yo] twice, k2tog, k1.

Rep rows 1-6.

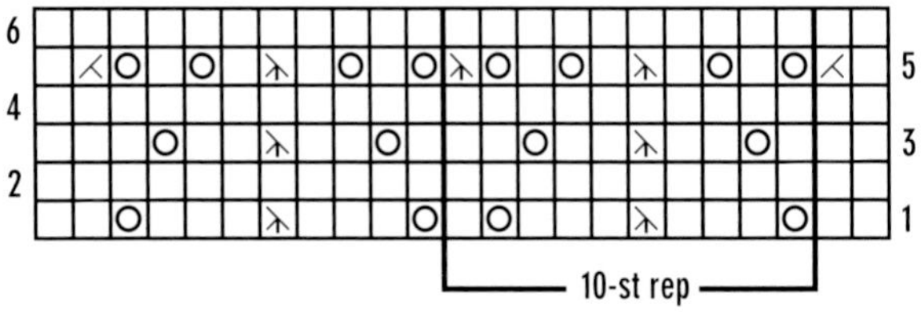

Stitch Key

K on RS, p on WS

K2tog

Yo

SK2P

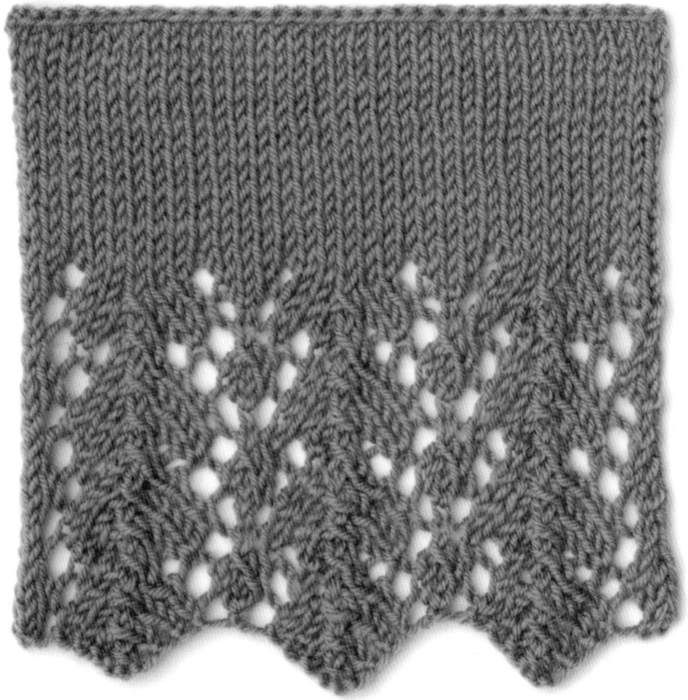

92

93 picot dots

(multiple of 5 sts plus 2)

Row 1 (RS) K1, yo, *k5, sl the 2nd, 3rd, 4th and 5th sts over first st, yo; rep from *, end k1.

Row 2 P1, *[p1, yo, k1 tbl] in yo, p1; rep from * to end.

Row 3 K2, k1 tbl, *k3, k1 tbl; rep from * to the last 2 sts, k2.

Row 4 Knit.

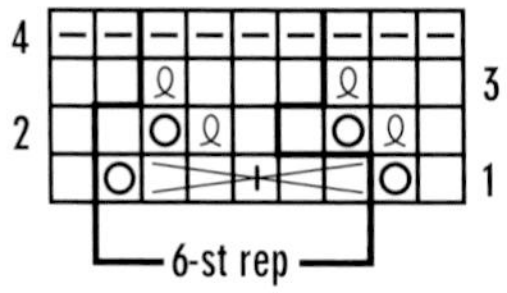

Stitch Key

K on RS, p on WS

P on RS, k on WS

Yo

K1 tbl on RS and WS

K5, sl the 2nd, 3rd, 4th and 5th st over the first st

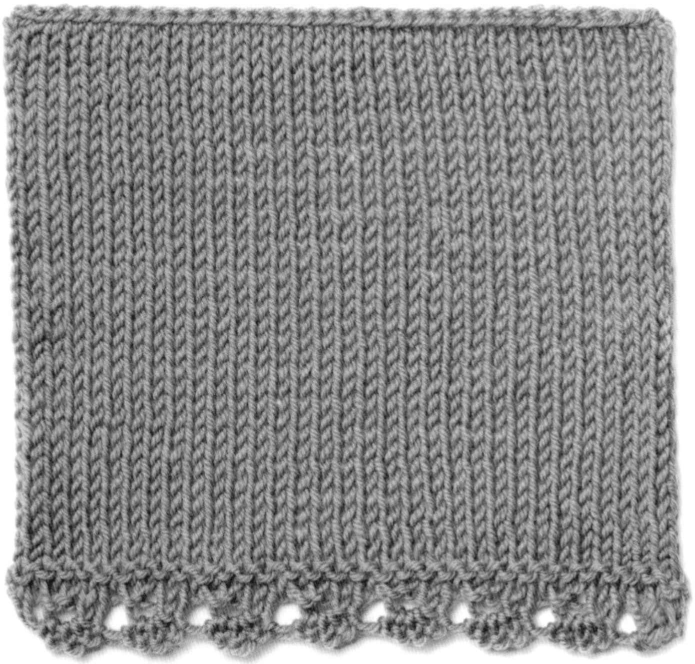

93

(multiple of 10 sts plus 2)

Row 1 (RS) K1, *k1, yo, k3, SK2P, k3, yo; rep from *, end k1.

Row 2 Knit.

Row 3 K1, *p1, k1, yo, k2, SK2P, k2, yo, k1; rep from *, end k1.

Rows 4, 6 and 8 P1, *p9, k1; rep from *, end p1.

Row 5 K1, *p1, k2, yo, k1, SK2P, k1, yo, k2; rep from *, end k1.

Row 7 K1, *p1, k3, yo, SK2P, yo, k3; rep from *, end k1.

Row 9 K1, *[k2tog, k3] twice; rep from *, end k1.

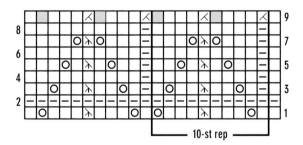

Stitch Key

☐	K on RS, p on WS
⊟	P on RS, k on WS
⊙	Yo
⟋	K2tog
⟑	SK2P
▨	No stitch

(multiple of 10 sts plus 4)

Row 1 (WS) Purl.

Row 2 K2, *yo, ssk, k8; rep from *, end k2.

Row 3 K2, *yo, p2tog, p5, p2tog tbl, yo, p1; rep from *, end k2.

Row 4 K4, *yo, ssk, k3, k2tog, yo, k3; rep from * to end.

Row 5 K2, p2, *yo, p2tog, p1, p2tog tbl, yo, p5; rep from *, end last rep p3, k2.

Row 6 K6, *yo, SK2P, yo, k7; rep from *, end last rep k5.

Row 7 K2, *p3, p2tog tbl, yo; rep from *, end k2.

Row 8 K3, *yo, ssk, k3; rep from *, end k1.

Row 9 K2, p1, *p2tog tbl, yo, p3; rep from *, end last rep p2, k2.

Row 10 K5, *yo, ssk, k3; rep from *, end k2.

Row 11 K1, *p2tog tbl, yo, p3; rep from *, end p1, k2.

Row 12 K2, *yo, ssk, k3; rep from *, end k2.

Rows 13, 14, 15 and 16 Rep rows 3, 4, 5 and 6.

Row 17 K2, p1, *p3, yo, p2tog; rep from *, end k1.

Row 18 K5, *k2tog, yo, k3; rep from *, end last rep k2.

Row 19 K2, p1, *yo, p2tog, p3; rep from *, end last rep p2, k2.

Row 20 K3, *k2tog, yo, k3; rep from *, end k1.

Row 21 K2, *p3, yo, p2tog; rep from *, end k2.

Row 22 K1, *k2tog, yo, k3; rep from *, end k3.

Rows 23, 24, 25 and 26 Rep rows 3, 4, 5 and 6.

Row 27 Purl.

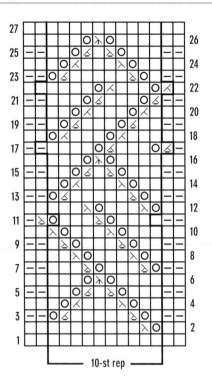

Stitch Key

☐	K on RS, p on WS
─	P on RS, k on WS
⟍	Ssk
⟋	K2tog
⊙	Yo
⟋	P2tog
⟍	P2tog tbl
⟑	SK2P

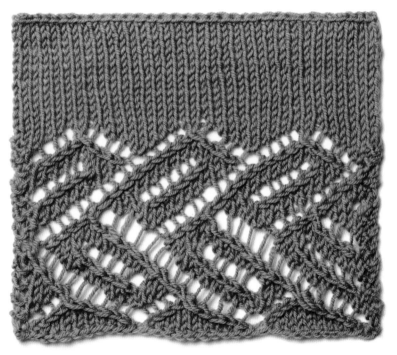

95

(multiple of 12 sts plus 3)

Set-up row Knit.

Row 1 (RS) K2, *yo, k4, SK2P, k4, yo, k1; rep from * to last st, k1.

Rows 2, 4, 6 and 8 Purl.

Row 3 K3, *yo, k3, SK2P, k3, yo, k3; rep from * to end.

Row 5 K4, *yo, k2, SK2P, k2, yo, k5; rep from * to last 11 sts, yo, k2, SK2P, k2, yo, k4.

Row 7 K5, *yo, k1, SK2P, k1, yo, k7; rep from * to last 10 sts, yo, k1, SK2P, k1, yo, k5.

Row 9 K6, *yo, SK2P, yo, k9; rep from * to last 9 sts, yo, SK2P, yo, k6.

Row 10 Purl.

Rows 11 and 12 Knit.

Rows 13, 14, 15 and 16 Rep rows 1–4.

Row 17 K1, k2tog, yo, k1, *yo, k2, SK2P, k2, yo, k1, yo, SK2P, yo, k1; rep from * to last 11 sts, yo, k2, SK2P, k2, yo, k1, yo, SKP, k1.

Rows 18 and 20 Purl.

Row 19 K1, k2tog, yo, k2, *yo, k1, SK2P, k1, yo, k2, yo, SK2P, yo, k2; rep from * to last 10 sts, yo, k1, SK2P, k1, yo, k2, yo, SKP, k1.

Row 21 K1, k2tog, yo, *k3, yo, SK2P, yo; rep from * to last 6 sts, k3, yo, SKP, k1.

Row 22 Purl.

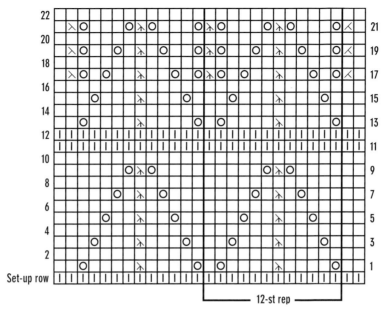

Stitch Key

☐ K on RS, p on WS
Ⅰ K on RS and on WS
Ⓞ Yo
◺ SKP
◹ K2tog
⋏ SK2P

(multiple of 14 sts plus 1)

Row 1 (RS) K6, *k2tog, yo, k5; rep from *, end k2.

Row 2 and all WS rows Purl.

Row 3 K1, *yo, ssk, k2, k2tog, yo, k1; rep from * to end.

Row 5 K2, *yo, ssk, k3, yo, ssk, k2, k2tog, yo, k3; rep from *, end last rep k2.

Row 7 K3, *yo, ssk, k5, k2tog, yo, k5; rep from *, end last rep k3.

Row 9 K2, *[yo, ssk] twice, k3, [k2tog, yo] twice, k3; rep from *, end last rep k2.

Row 11 Rep row 7.

Row 13 K4, *yo, ssk, k3, k2tog, yo, k7; rep from *, end last rep k4.

Row 15 K5, *yo, ssk, k1, k2tog, yo, k3, k2tog, yo, k4; rep from *, end yo, ssk, k1, k2tog, yo, k5.

Row 17 K1, *yo, ssk, k3, yo, Sk2P, yo, k3, k2tog, yo, k1; rep from * to end.

Row 19 K7, *yo, ssk, k5; rep from *, end k1.

Row 21 Knit.

Row 22 Purl.

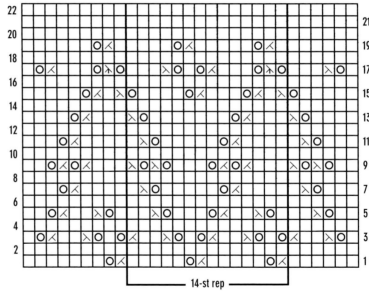

Stitch Key

☐ K on RS, p on WS

⊙ Yo

⊠ Ssk

⊠ K2tog

⧄ SK2P

14-st rep

98 waves of grain

(worked over 6 sts)

Note Sts for St st were picked up after edging was knit.

Cast on 6 sts.

Row 1 (RS) K2, yo, k2tog, yo, k2—7 sts.

Rows 2, 4, 6 and 8 Knit.

Row 3 K3, yo, k2tog, yo, k2—8 sts.

Row 5 K4, yo, k2tog, yo, k2—9 sts.

Row 7 K5, yo, k2tog, yo, k2—10 sts.

Row 9 K6, yo, k2tog, yo, k2—11 sts.

Row 10 Bind off 5 sts, k to end—6 sts.

Rep rows 1–10.

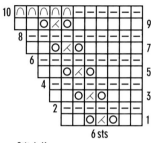

6 sts

Stitch Key

☐ K on RS, p on WS

⊟ P on RS, k on WS

⊙ Yo

⊠ K2tog

⌒ Bind off 1 st

99 periwinkles

(worked over 3 sts)

Note Sts for St st were picked up after edging was knit.

Cast on 3 sts.

Row 1 (RS) Knit.

Row 2 K1, yo 6 times, k2.

Row 3 K2, in yo's work [k1, p1] 3 times dropping all yo's, k1.

Rows 4 and 5 Knit.

Row 6 K1, [yo, k2tog] 4 times.

Rows 7 and 8 Knit.

Row 9 Bind off 6 sts, k to end.

Rep rows 2–9.

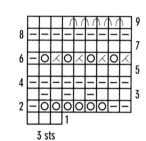

3 sts

Stitch Key

☐ K on RS, p on WS

⊟ P on RS, k on WS

⊙ Yo

⊠ K2tog

⌒ Bind off 6 sts

lace

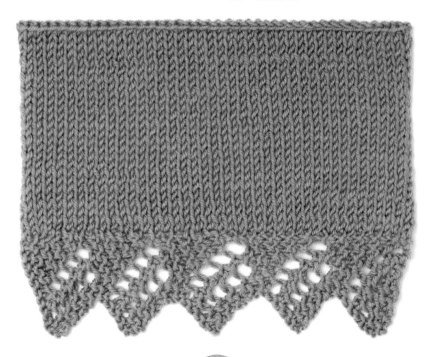

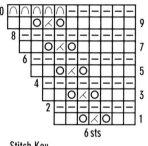

98

99

S2KP Sl 2 sts tog as if to k2tog, k1, pass the 2 sl sts over the k1.

(worked over 9 sts)

Note Sts for St st were picked up after edging was knit.

Cast on 9 sts.

Row 1 (RS) Yo, k2tog, yo, k1, yo, ssk, k4.

Row 2 P5, k5.

Row 3 Yo, k2tog, yo, k3, yo, ssk, k3.

Row 4 P4, k7.

Row 5 Yo, k2tog, yo, k2, ssk, k1, yo, ssk, k2.

Row 6 P3, k1, ssk, yo 3 times, k2tog, k3.

Row 7 Yo, k2tog, yo, ssk, p1, k1, p1, k2tog, yo, k3.

Row 8 P4, k5, k2tog, k1.

Row 9 Yo, k2tog, yo, ssk, k1, k2tog, yo, k4.

Row 10 P5, k3, k2tog, k1.

Row 11 Yo, k2tog, yo, S2KP, yo, k5.

Row 12 P6, k1, k2tog, k1.

Rep rows 1–12.

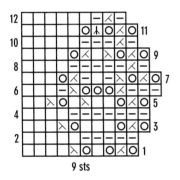

9 sts

Stitch Key

☐ K on RS, p on WS

⊟ P on RS, k on WS

⧄ SKP

⧅ K2tog

⼊ S2KP

⊙ Yo

(worked over 6 sts)

Note Sts for St st were picked up after edging was knit.

Row 1 (RS) K1, k2tog, yo, k2, yo twice, k1—8 sts.

Row 2 K2, knit into back loop of 2nd yo, k2tog, yo, k3.

Row 3 K1, k2tog, yo, k5.

Row 4 Bind off 2 sts, k2tog, yo, k3—6 sts.

Rep rows 1–4.

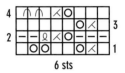

6 sts

Stitch Key

☐ K on RS, p on WS

⧅ K1 tbl on RS

⊙ Yo

⧅ K2tog

⌒ Bind off 2 sts

102 victorian lace II

(worked over 6 sts)

Note Sts for St st were picked up after edging was knit.

Cast on 6 sts.

Row 1 (RS) K1, k2tog, yo, k2, yo twice, k1—8 sts.

Row 2 P1, p into front and back of double yo, p2tog, yo, p3.

Row 3 K1, k2tog, yo, k5.

Row 4 Bind off first 2 sts, p2tog, yo, p3—6 sts.

Rep rows 1-4.

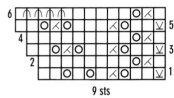

Stitch Key

☐ K on RS, p on WS

⌾ P1 tbl on WS

⚬ Yo

⟋ K2tog

⟍ P2tog

⌒ Bind off 2 sts

102

103 band of lace

(worked over 19 sts)

Note Sts for St st were picked up after edging was knit.

Cast on 9 sts.

Row 1 (RS) Sl 1, k2, yo, k2tog, k1, yo, k1, yo, k2—11 sts.

Row 2 K8, yo, k2tog, k1.

Row 3 Sl 1, k2, yo, k2tog, k2, yo, k2tog, yo, k2—12 sts.

Row 4 K9, yo, k2tog, k1.

Row 5 Sl 1, k2, yo, k2tog, k3, yo, k2tog, yo, k2—13 sts.

Row 6 Bind off 4 sts, k5, yo, k2tog, k1.

Rep rows 1-6.

Stitch Key

☐ K on RS, p on WS

— P on RS, k on WS

⚬ Yo

⟋ K2tog

⌒ Bind off 4

⌵ Sl st purlwise wyib

103

lace

77

(beg as a multiple of 19 sts plus 2, end as a multiple of 19 plus 1)

Rows 1, 3, 5 and 7 (RS) K1, *SKP, k3, [yo, SKP] twice, yo, k1, yo, [k2tog, yo] twice, k3, k2tog; rep from *, end k1.

Row 2 and all WS rows Purl.

Row 9 K1, *SKP, k2, [yo, k2tog] twice, yo, k3, yo, [SKP, yo] twice, k2, k2tog; rep from *, end k1.

Row 11 K1, *SKP, k1, [yo, k2tog] twice, yo, k5, yo, [SKP, yo] twice, k1, k2tog; rep from *, end k1.

Row 13 K1, *SKP, k1, [yo, k2tog] twice, yo, k7, yo, [SKP, yo] twice, k2tog; rep from *, end k1.

Row 15 (*Note* the last sl st is the st that will be passed over in the k1 at the beg of the next rep for a SKP.)
Sl 1, k1, pass sl st over k1, [yo, k2tog] twice, yo, k3, k2tog, k4, yo, [SKP, yo] twice, sl 1, *k1, pass over the sl-st from previous pattern repeat, [yo, k2tog] twice, yo, k3, k2tog, k4, yo, [SKP, yo] twice, sl 1; rep from *, end last rep SKP.

Rows 17, 19, 21 and 23 K1, *[yo, k2tog] twice, yo, k3, k2tog, SKP, k3, yo, [SKP, yo] twice, k1; rep from * to end.

Row 25 K1, *k1, [yo, SKP] twice, yo, k2, k2tog, SKP, k2, [yo, k2tog] twice, yo, k2; rep from * to end.

Row 27 K1, *k2, [yo, SKP] twice, yo, k1, k2tog, SKP, k1, yo, [k2tog, yo] twice, k3; rep from * to end.

Row 29 K1, *k3, [yo, SKP] twice, yo, k2tog, SKP, yo, [k2tog, yo] twice, k4; rep from * to end.

Row 31 K1, *k4, [yo, SKP] twice, yo, SKP, yo, [k2tog, yo] twice, k3, k2tog; rep from * to end.

Stitch Key

☐ K on RS, p on WS	⊠ K2tog
⊠ SKP	⊙ Yo

19-st rep

SK2P Sl 1, k2tog, psso.

(multiple of 18 sts plus 2)

Note Sts for St st were picked up after edging was knit.

Cast on 20 sts.

Row 1 and all WS rows Purl.

Row 2 P2, *k9, yo, k1, yo, k3, SK2P, p2; rep from * to end.

Row 4 P2, *k10, yo, k1, yo, k2, SK2P, p2; rep from * to end.

Row 6 P2, *k3tog, k4, yo, k1, yo, k3, [yo, k1] twice, SK2P, p2; rep from * to end.

Row 8 P2, *k3tog, k3, yo, k1, yo, k9, p2; rep from * to end.

Row 10 P2, *k3tog, k2, yo, k1, yo, k10, p2; rep from * to end.

Row 12 P2, *k3tog, [k1, yo] twice, k3, yo, k1, yo, k4, SK2P, p2; rep from * to end.

Rep rows 1–12.

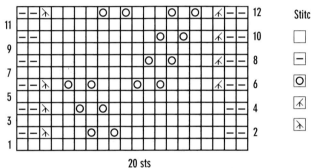

Stitch Key

☐ K on RS, p on WS

– P on RS, k on WS

O Yo

⋏ K3tog

⋏ SK2P

20 sts

SK2P Sl 1, k2tog, psso.

Cross Dec (CD) Sl 1 to cn and hold to *back*, sl 1, return first st to LH needle, k2tog, psso.

(multiple of 14 sts plus 13)

Row 1 (RS) [K1, p1] 6 times, k1, *[yo, k1] twice, [p1, k1] 6 times; rep from * to end.

Row 2 *[P1, k1] 6 times, p4; rep from *, end [p1, k1] 6 times, p1.

Row 3 [K1, p1] 6 times, k1, *yo, k3, yo, [k1, p1] 6 times, k1; rep from * to end.

Row 4 *[P1, k1] 6 times, p6; rep from *, end [p1, k1] 6 times, p1.

Row 5 [K1, p1] 6 times, k1, *yo, k1, k2tog, yo, k2, yo, [k1, p1] 6 times, k1; rep from * to end.

Row 6 *[P1, k1] 6 times, p8; rep from *, end [p1, k1] 6 times, p1.

Row 7 [K1, p1] 6 times, k1, *yo, k1, k2tog, yo, k1, yo, ssk, k1, yo, [k1, p1] 6 times, k1; rep from * to end.

Row 8 *[P1, k1] 6 times, p10; rep from *, end [p1, k1] 6 times, p1.

Row 9 [K1, p1] 3 times, k1, CD, k3tog, *k10, k3tog, CD twice, SK2P; rep from *, end last rep k, SK2P, k3tog, [k1, p1] 3 times, k1.

These 9 rows form pat.

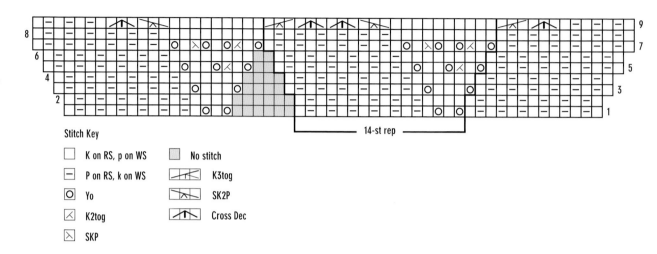

Stitch Key

□	K on RS, p on WS	▨	No stitch
─	P on RS, k on WS	⟋	K3tog
○	Yo	⟍	SK2P
⟋	K2tog	⟰	Cross Dec
⟍	SKP		

14-st rep

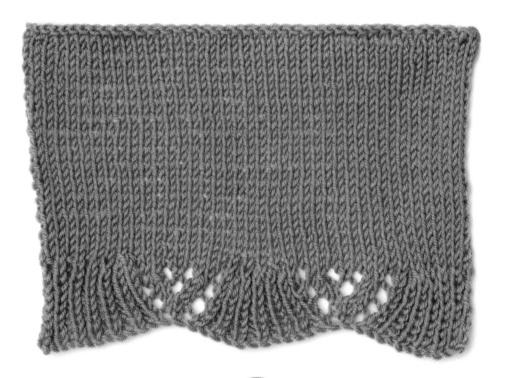

(worked over 12 sts)

Note Sts for St st were picked up after edging was knit.

Note Work yo twice as 2 sts on the foll row.

Cast on 12 sts.

Row 1 (RS) K5, yo, k2tog, k5.

Row 2 [K2tog, yo twice] twice, k3, yo, k2tog, k1, p2 — 14 sts.

Row 3 K5, yo, k2tog, [k2, p1] twice, k1.

Row 4 [K2tog, yo twice] twice, k5, yo, k2tog, k1, p2 — 16 sts.

Row 5 K5, yo, k2tog, k4, p1, k2, p1, k1.

Row 6 [K2tog, yo twice] twice, k7, yo, k2tog, k1, p2 — 18 sts.

Row 7 K5, yo, k2tog, k6, p1, k2, p1, k1.

Row 8 Bind off 6 sts knitwise, k to last 5 sts, yo, k2tog, k1, p2 — 12 sts.

Rep rows 1–8.

12 sts

Stitch Key

☐ K on RS, p on WS

⊟ P on RS, k on WS

⊡ Yo

⊠ K2tog

⌒ Bind off 6 sts knitwise

4-st Wrap (WS) P4, sl these sts to dpn and hold away from needles, wrap yarn counterclockwise 3 times, return sts to RH needle.

(multiple of 21 sts plus 3)

Rows 1 and 3 (WS) Knit.

Row 2 Purl.

Row 4 K1, *yo, k21; rep from *, end k2.

Row 5 P2, * p1, [k3, p1] 5 times, p1; rep from *, end p1.

Row 6 K1, *k1, yo, k1, [p3, k1] 5 times, yo; rep from *, end k2.

Row 7 P2, *p2, [k3, p1] 5 times, p2; rep from *, end p1.

Row 8 K1, *[k1, yo] twice, [ssk, p2] 5 times, [k1, yo] twice; rep from *, end k2.

Row 9 P2, *p4, [k2, p1] 5 times, p4; rep from *, end p1.

Row 10 K1, *[k1, yo] 4 times, [ssk, p1] 5 times, [k1, yo] 4 times; rep from *, end k2.

Row 11 P2, *p8, [k1, p1] 5 times, p8; rep from *, end p1.

Row 12 K1, *k8, ssk 5 times, k8; rep from *, end k2.

Row 13 P2, *p8, 4-st wrap, p9; rep from *, end p1.

Row 14 Knit.

Rep rows 1–14.

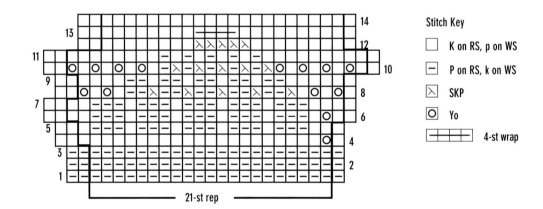

Stitch Key

☐ K on RS, p on WS

— P on RS, k on WS

⊠ SKP

⊙ Yo

▭ 4-st wrap

109 ballroom girls

S2KP Sl 2 sts, k1, psso.

Cluster Sl the given number of sts wyib, pass yarn to front of work, sl the same number of sts back to LH needle, pass yarn to back of work, sl the same sts again wyib.
(multiple of 22 sts plus 1)

Row 1 (RS) K1, *yo, [k1 tbl, p3] 5 times, k1 tbl, yo, k1; rep from * to end.

Row 2 P3, *[k3, p1] 4 times, k3, p5; rep from *, end last rep p3.

Row 3 K1, *yo, k1 tbl, yo, [k1 tbl, p3] 5 times, [k1 tbl, yo] twice, k1; rep from * to end.

Row 4 P5, *[k3, p1] 4 times, k3, p9; rep from *, end last rep p5.

Row 5 K1, *yo, k1 tbl, yo, k2tog tbl, yo, [k1 tbl, p2tog, p1] 5 times, k1 tbl, yo, k2tog, yo, k1 tbl, yo, k1; rep from * to end.

Row 6 P7, *[k2, p1] 4 times, k2, p13; rep from *, end last rep p7.

Row 7 K1, *k1 tbl, [yo, k2tog tbl] twice, yo, [k1 tbl, p2] 5 times, k1 tbl, yo, [k2tog, yo] twice, k1 tbl, k1; rep from * to end.

Row 8 P8, *[k2, p1] 4 times, k2, p15; rep from *, end last rep p8.

Row 9 K2, *[yo, k2tog] twice, yo, k1 tbl, yo, [k1 tbl, p2tog] 5 times, [k1 tbl, yo] twice, [k2tog tbl, yo] twice, k3; rep from *, end last rep k2.

Row 10 P10, *[k1, p1] 4 times, k1, p19; rep from *, end last rep p10.

Row 11 K2tog tbl, *[yo, k2tog] 3 times, k1 tbl, yo, [k1 tbl, p1] 5 times, k1 tbl, yo, k1 tbl, [k2tog tbl, yo] 3 times, S2KP; rep from *, end last rep k2tog.

Row 12 Rep row 10.

Row 13 K1, *[k2tog, yo] twice, k2tog, k1, k1 tbl, yo, k2tog tbl twice, SK2P, k2tog twice, yo, k1 tbl, k1, k2tog tbl, [yo, k2tog tbl] twice, k1; rep from * to end.

Row 14 Cluster 2, *p7, cluster 5, p7, cluster 3; rep from *, end last rep cluster 2.

Rep rows 1–14.

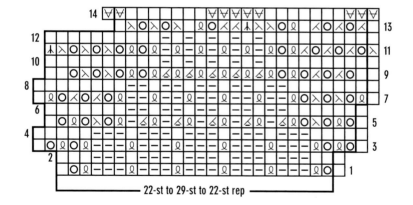

Stitch Key

□	K on RS, p on WS
−	P on RS, k on WS
ℚ	K1 tbl
○	Yo
⟍	K2tog tbl
⟋	K2tog
⟋	P2tog
⋏	S2KP (end last rep on row 11, k2tog)
⩝	Cluster

22-st to 29-st to 22-st rep

113 bear claw

(worked over 8 sts)

Note Sts for St st were picked up after edging was knit.

Cast on 8 sts and knit 1 row.

Row 1 Sl 1, k1, [yo, k2tog] twice, yo, k2 — 9 sts.

Row 2 K2, yo, k2, [yo, k2tog] twice, k1 — 10 sts.

Row 3 Sl 1, k1, [yo, k2tog] twice, k2, yo, k2 — 11 sts.

Row 4 K2, yo, k4, [yo, k2tog] twice, k1 — 12 sts.

Row 5 Sl 1, k1, [yo, k2tog] twice, k4, yo, k2 — 13 sts.

Row 6 K2, yo, k6, [yo, k2tog] twice, k1 — 14 sts.

Row 7 Sl 1, k1, [yo, k2tog] twice, k6, yo, k2 — 15 sts.

Row 8 K2, yo, k8, [yo, k2tog] twice, k1 — 16 sts.

Row 9 Sl 1, k1, [yo, k2tog] twice, k8, yo, k2 — 17 sts.

Row 10 K2, yo, k10, [yo, k2tog] twice, k1 — 18 sts.

Row 11 Sl 1, k1, [yo, k2tog] twice, k10, yo, k2 — 19 sts.

Row 12 Bind off 11 sts, k2, [yo, k2tog] twice, k1 — 8 sts.

Rep rows 1-12.

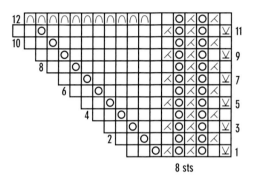

Stitch Key

☐ K on RS, p on WS

☒ SKP

☒ K2tog

⊡ Yo

☒ Sl st

⌒ Bind off 11 sts

8 sts

SK2P Sl 1, k2tog, pass the sl st over the k2tog.

(worked over 8 sts)

Note Sts for St st were picked up after edging was knit.

Cast on 8 sts.

Row 1 Yo, p2tog, (k1, p1, k1, p1, k1) in next st, yo, p2tog, k1, yo 3 times, k2 – 15 sts.

Row 2 K3, p1, k2, yo, p2tog, k5, yo, p2tog.

Row 3 Yo, p2tog, k5, yo, p2tog, k6.

Row 4 K6, yo, p2tog, k5, yo, p2tog.

Row 5 Yo, p2tog, ssk, k1, k2tog, yo, k2tog, k6 – 13 sts.

Row 6 Bind off 3 sts, k2, yo, p2tog, SK2P, yo, p2tog – 8 sts.

Rep rows 1–6.

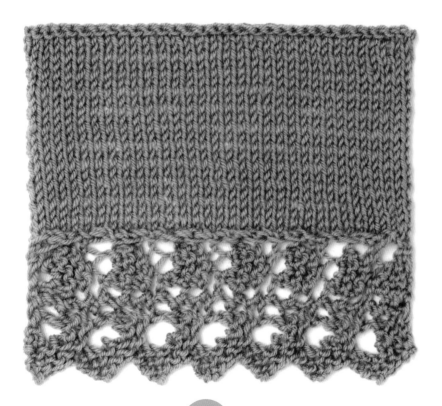

8 sts

Stitch Key

☐ K on RS, p on WS

— P on RS, k on WS

⊙ Yo

◿ K2tog

◺ SKP

◿ P2tog

⤴ SK2P

⌒ Bind off 3 sts

lace

(worked over 10 sts)

Note Sts for St st were picked up after edging was knit.

Cast on 10 sts and k 1 row.

Row 1 (RS) Sl 1, k1, [yo, k2tog] twice, yo 4 times, k2tog, yo, p2tog.

Row 2 Yo, p2tog, k1, [k1, p1] twice into the yo 4 times, [k1, p1] twice, k2.

Row 3 Sl 1, [k1, yo, k2tog] twice, k4, yo, p2tog.

Row 4 Yo, p2tog, k5, [p1, k2] twice.

Row 5 Sl 1, k1, yo, k2tog, k2, yo, k2tog, k3, yo, p2tog.

Row 6 Yo, p2tog, k4, p1, k3, p1, k2.

Row 7 Sl 1, k1, yo, k2tog, k3, yo, k2tog, k2, yo, p2tog.

Row 8 Yo, p2tog, k3, p1, k4, p1, k2.

Row 9 Sl 1, k1, yo, k2tog, k4, yo, k2tog, k1, yo, p2tog.

Row 10 Yo, p2tog, k2, p1, k5, p1, k2.

Row 11 Sl 1, k1, yo, k2tog, k5, yo, k2tog, yo, p2tog.

Row 12 Bind off 3 sts, then slip the st from RH needle back to LH needle, yo, p2tog, k5, p1, k2.

Rep rows 1–12.

Stitch Key

☐ K on RS, p on WS

☐ P on RS, k on WS

☐ Yo

☐ K2tog

☐ P2tog

☐ Sl 1

☐ Bind off 3 sts

10 sts

(worked over 23 sts)

Note Sts for St st were picked up after edging was knit.

Cast on 23 sts.

Row 1 (RS) K2, yo, [k2tog, yo] 4 times, k2, SK2P, yo twice, k2, k2tog, yo, k4.

Row 2 K2, k2tog, yo, k4, p1 and k1 into double yo, k12, k2tog, yo.

Row 3 K1 tbl into yo, k1, yo, [k2tog, yo] 4 times, k2, k2tog, k4, k2tog, yo, k4.

Row 4 K2, k2tog, yo, k18, k2tog, yo.

Row 5 K1 tbl into yo, k1, yo, [k2tog, yo] 4 times, k1, SK2P, yo twice, k2tog, yo twice, k2, k2tog, yo, k4.

Row 6 K2, k2tog, yo, k4, [p1 and k1 into double yo, k1] twice, k10, k2tog, yo.

Row 7 K1 tbl into yo, k1, yo, [k2tog, yo] 4 times, k10, k2tog, yo, k4.

Row 8 K2, k2tog, yo, k21, k2tog, yo.

Row 9 K1 tbl into yo, k1, yo, [k2tog, yo] 4 times, k1, [SK2P, yo twice] 2 times, k2tog, yo twice, k2, k2tog, yo, k4.

Row 10 K2, k2tog, yo, k4, [p1 and k1 into double yo, k1] 3 times, k10, k2tog, yo.

Row 11 K1 tbl into yo, k1, yo, [k2tog, yo] 4 times, k13, k2tog, yo, k4.

Row 12 K2, k2tog, yo, k24, k2tog, yo.

Row 13 K1 tbl into yo, k1, yo, [k2tog, yo] 4 times, k1, [SK2P, yo twice] 3 times, k2tog, yo twice, k2, k2tog, yo, k4.

Row 14 K2, k2tog, yo, k4, [p1 and k1 into double yo, k1] 4 times, k10, k2tog, yo.

Row 15 K1 tbl into yo, k1, yo, [k2tog, yo] 4 times, k16, k2tog, yo, k4.

Row 16 K2, k2tog, yo, k27, k2tog, yo—33 sts.

Row 17 Bind off 10 sts, k until there are 17 sts on RH needle, k2tog, yo, k4—23 sts.

Row 18 K2 k2tog, yo, k17, k2tog, yo.

Rep rows 1–18.

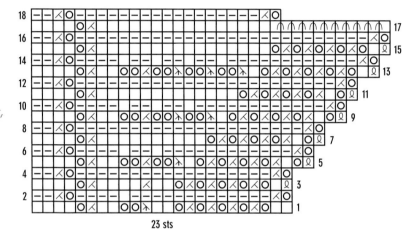

23 sts

Stitch Key

☐ K on RS, p on WS

⊟ P on RS, k on WS

⊡ Yo

⊠ K2tog

↗ SK2P

⊠ K1 tbl on RS

⌒ Bind off 10 sts

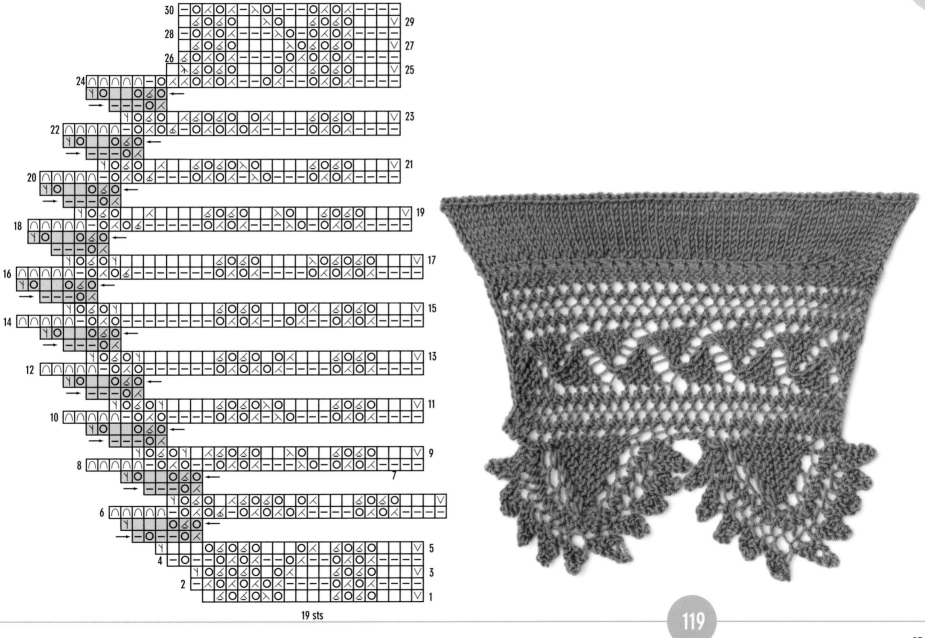

19 sts

119

LS (over 5 sts) Yo, k2tog, k1, ssk, yo.

Note Sts for St st were picked up after edging was knit.

(worked over 30 sts)

Cast on 30 sts.

Row 1 (RS) Yo, k2tog, k1, yo, k3, LS, [k1, yo, ssk, k1, k2tog, yo] twice, k1, LS, ssk, turn.

Row 2 and all WS rows Sl 1, p to last 2 sts, k2.

Row 3 Yo, k2tog, k1, yo, k4, LS, [k1, yo, k1, sk2p, k1, yo] twice, k1, LS, ssk, turn.

*Row 5 Yo, k2tog, k2, yo, k2, k2tog, yo, k1, LS, [k1, k2tog, yo, k1, yo, ssk] twice, k1, LS, ssk, turn.

Row 7 Yo, k2tog, k1, yo, k2, k2tog, yo, k2, LS, k2tog, k1, [yo, k1] twice, sk2p, [k1, yo] twice, k1, ssk, turn.

Row 9 Yo, k2tog, k1, yo, k2, k2tog, yo, k3, LS, [k1, yo, ssk, k1, k2tog, yo] twice, k1, LS, ssk, turn.

Row 11 Yo, k2tog, k1, yo, k2, k2tog, yo, k4, LS, [k1, yo, k1, sk2p, k1, yo] twice, k1, LS, ssk, turn.

Row 13 Yo, k2tog, ssk, yo, ssk, k2, yo, ssk, k2, LS, [k1, k2tog, yo, k1, yo, ssk] twice, k1, LS, ssk, turn.

Row 15 Yo, k2tog, ssk, yo, ssk k2, ssk, k1, LS, k2tog, [k1, yo] twice, k1, sk2p, [k1, yo] twice, k1, ssk, LS, ssk, turn.

Row 17 Yo, k2tog, ssk, yo, ssk k2, yo, ssk, LS, [k1, yo, ssk, k1, k2tog, yo] twice, k1, LS, ssk, turn.

Row 19 Yo, k2tog, ssk, yo, ssk k3, LS, [k1, yo, k1, sk2p, k1, yo] twice, LS, ssk, turn.

Row 21 Yo, k2tog, ssk, yo, ssk k2, LS, [k1, k2tog, yo, k1, yo, ssk] twice, k1, LS, ssk, turn.

Row 23 Yo, k2tog, ssk, yo, ssk k1, LS, k2tog, [k1, yo] twice, k1, sk2p, [k1, yo] twice, k1, ssk, LS, ssk, turn.

Row 24 Rep row 2.

Rep rows 1–24.

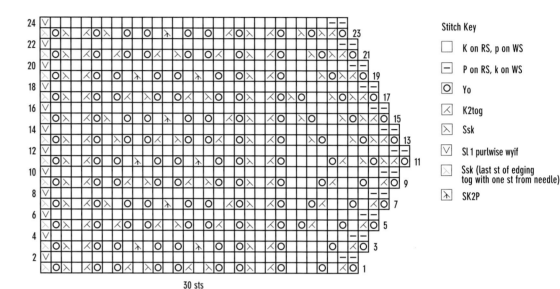

30 sts

Stitch Key

☐ K on RS, p on WS

▬ P on RS, k on WS

⊙ Yo

⊠ K2tog

⊠ Ssk

⋁ Sl 1 purlwise wyif

⊠ Ssk (last st of edging tog with one st from needle)

⋏ SK2P

121 double trellis

S2KP Sl 2, k1, pass the 2 sl sts over the k1.
(multiple of 15 sts plus 4)
Knit 1 row.

Next 3 rows K2, *inc in next st, k5, S2KP, k5, inc in
next st; rep from * to last 2 sts, k4.

Next row Knit.

Row 1 (RS) K4, *[yo, ssk] twice, S2KP, [yo, k2tog]
twice, yo, k1, p2, k1; rep from * to last 15 sts, [yo, ssk]
twice, yo, S2KP, [yo, k2tog] twice, yo, k4.

Rows 2 and 4 K3, *p13, k2; rep from * to last 16 sts,
p13, k3.

Row 3 K3, *[yo, ssk] 3 times, k1, [k2tog, yo] 3 times,
p2; rep from * to last 16 sts, [yo, ssk] 3 times, k1,
[k2tog, yo] 3 times, k3.

Rep rows 1–4.

Next 3 rows K2, *inc in next st, k5, S2KP, k5, inc in
next st; rep from * to last 2 sts, k4.

Next row Knit.

Work 4 rows of trellis pat 6 times, end with row 3.
Break yarn.

Cast on and work 4 row of trellis pat twice, end
with row 3.

Next (joining) row With needles parallel, WS facing
and using a 3rd needle, work row 4 of trellis pat,
working sts tog from both needles. Cont in trellis pat.

Stitch Key

☐ K on RS, p on WS

─ P on RS, k on WS

⟍ SKP

⟋ K2tog

⋏ S2KP

○ Yo

15-st rep

color

122 garter stripes

Rows 1 and 2 With A, knit.
Rows 3 and 4 With C, knit.
Rows 5 and 6 With A, knit.
Rows 7 and 8 With B, knit.
Rep rows 1–8 once more.

123 welted stripes

Row 1 (RS) With B, knit.
Row 2 Knit.
Row 3 Purl.
Row 4 Knit.
Rows 5, 7 and 9 With A, knit.
Rows 6, 8 and 10 Purl.
Rep rows 1–10.

122

123

124 ribbed stripes

Work in k1, p1 rib as foll:
2 rows A
1 row B
1 row C
2 rows A
1 row D
1 row E
2 rows A
1 row F
1 row G
2 rows A

125 feather and fan

(multiple of 18 sts)
Cast on with CC.
Beg with a WS row and k 1 row, p 1 row, k 1 row.
Change to MC.
Rows 1 (RS) Knit.
Rows 2 and 4 Purl.
Row 3 *[K2tog] 3 times, [yo, k1] 6 times, [k2tog] 3 times; rep
from * to end.
Rep rows 1–4 three times.
Change to CC. K 2 rows, p 1 row, k 1 row.

color

124

125

126 striped scallops

(multiple of 18 st plus 2)
Row 1 (RS) With D, knit.
Row 2 With D, knit.
Row 3 With C, k1, *[k2tog] 3 times, [yo, k1] 6 times,
[k2tog] 3 times; rep from *, end k1.
Row 4 With C, knit.
Row 5 With B, knit.
Row 6 With B, knit.

Row 7 With E, k1, *[k2tog] 3 times, [yo, k1] 6 times,
[k2tog] 3 times; rep from *, end k1.
Row 8 With E, knit.
Row 9 (RS) With F, knit.
Row 10 With F, knit.
Row 11 With A, k1, *[k2tog] 3 times, [yo, k1] 6 times,
[k2tog] 3 times; rep from *, end k1.
Row 12 With A, knit.

126

127 vertical stripes

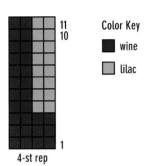

11
10

1

4-st rep

Color Key

■ wine

▨ lilac

128 1x1 corrugated rib

(multiple of 2 sts plus 1)

Prep Row With MC, *k1, p1; rep from *, end k1.

Row 1 (RS) *P1 MC, k1 A; rep from *, end p1 MC.

Row 2 *K1 MC, p1 A; rep from *, end k1 MC.

Rep rows 1 and 2.

color

127

128

129 1x1 corrugated rib II

(over an odd number of sts)
Row 1 (RS) *K1 A, p1 MC; rep from *, end k1 A.
Row 2 *P1 A, k1 MC; rep from *, end p1 A.
Rep rows 1 and 2.

130 2x2 corrugated rib

(multiple of 4 sts)
Cast on with MC.
P 1 row. K 1 row.
Row 1 (RS) K3 MC, *k2 CC, k2 MC; rep from *, end k1 MC.
Row 2 P3 MC, *k2 CC, p2 MC; rep from *, end p1 MC.
Row 3 K3 MC, *p2 CC, k2 MC; rep from *, end k1 MC.
Rep rows 2 and 3.

129

130

131 cabled stripes

132 textured stripes

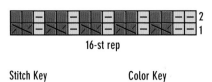

16-st rep

Stitch Key

☐ K on RS, P on WS

⊟ P on RS, K on WS

⊠ LT

Color Key

▨ ecru

▨ magenta

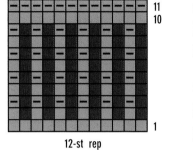

12-st rep

Stitch Key

☐ K on RS, p on WS

⊟ P on RS, k on WS

Color Key

▨ rose

■ wine

131

132

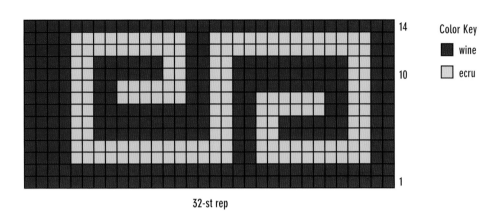

32-st rep

Color Key

■ wine

□ ecru

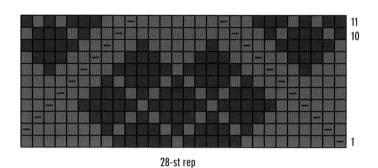

28-st rep

Stitch Key

□ K on RS, p on WS

⊟ P on RS, k on WS

Color Key

■ Rose

■ Wine

133

134

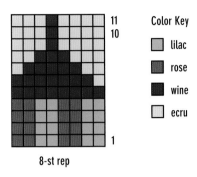

11
10

1

8-st rep

Color Key

lilac

rose

wine

ecru

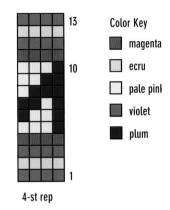

13

10

1

4-st rep

Color Key

magenta

ecru

pale pink

violet

plum

135

136

137 boxcars

10

1

8-st rep

Stitch Key

☐ K on RS, p on WS

⊟ P on RS, k on WS

Color Key

■ violet

■ plum

■ lilac

■ magenta

138 bobble balloons

MB (make bobble)
Row 1 (WS) P1.
Row 2 K into front, back and front of st.
Row 3 P3.
Row 4 K3.
Row 5 P3.
Row 6 SK2P.
(multiple of 6 sts plus 2)
Cast on with MC.
Rows 1 and 3 (RS) P2, *k1, p2; rep from * to end.
Rows 2 and 4 K2, *p1, k2; rep from * to end.

Row 5 Knit.
Row 6 *K2 MC, MB with A, k2 MC, p1 MC; rep from *, end k2 MC.
Work 5 rows more in rib pat in colors as established, working rows 2-6 of bobble pat on A sts.
With MC rib 2 rows.
Next row (WS) *K2 MC, p1 MC, k2 MC, MB with B; rep from *, end k2 MC.
Work 5 rows more in rib pat in colors as established, working rows 2-6 of bobble pat on B sts.
With MC rib 2 rows.

137

138

139 flower band

Work 8-st flowers in colors as desired.

Cast on 14 sts.

Work in k1, p1 rib for 1½"/4cm.

*Work 12 rows of flower chart as foll: Rib 3 sts, work chart over 8 sts, rib 3 sts.

Rib 12 rows; rep from * for desired length.

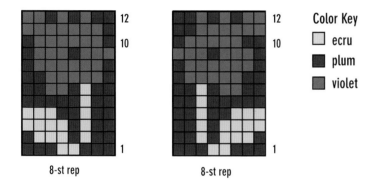

8-st rep   8-st rep

Color Key

☐ ecru

■ plum

■ violet

139

140 snowflakes

(multiple of 12 sts)

Row 1 (RS) K1, ssk, *k9, sl 2, k1, p2sso; rep from * to last 12 sts, end k9, k2tog, k1.

Row 2 K1, *p1, k4, (k1, yo, k1) all in 1 st, k4; rep from * to last 2 sts, end p1, k1.

Rep rows 1 and 2 four times for chevron border.

Work chart for 13 rows.

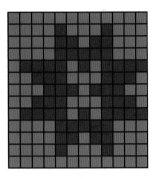

Color Key

■ magenta

■ wine

12-st rep

141 checker cab

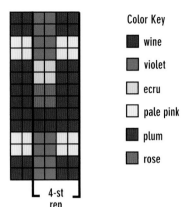

Color Key

■ wine

■ violet

■ ecru

□ pale pink

■ plum

■ rose

4-st rep

Stitch Key

☐ K on RS, p on WS

⊟ P on RS, k on WS

Color Key

▨ magenta

■ plum

■ wine

▨ violet

32
30
20
10
1

8-st rep

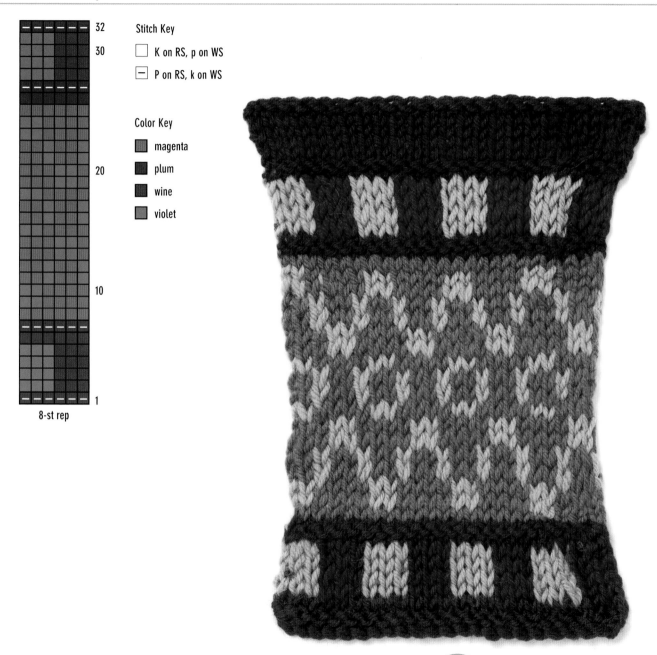

143 byzantine band

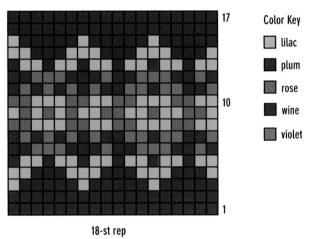

Color Key

- ☐ lilac
- ■ plum
- ■ rose
- ■ wine
- ■ violet

18-st rep

143

Color Key

■ plum
□ lilac

29

20

10

1

39-st rep

145 paint palette

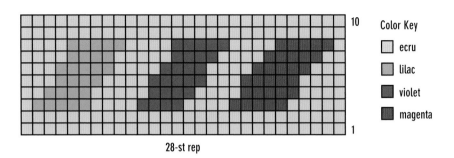

28-st rep

Color Key

☐ ecru

▨ lilac

▨ violet

▨ magenta

146 checkerboard

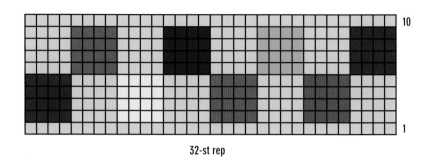

32-st rep

Color Key

☐ ecru   ▨ wine

▨ magenta   ▨ lilac

▨ rose   ▨ plum

☐ pale pink   ▨ violet

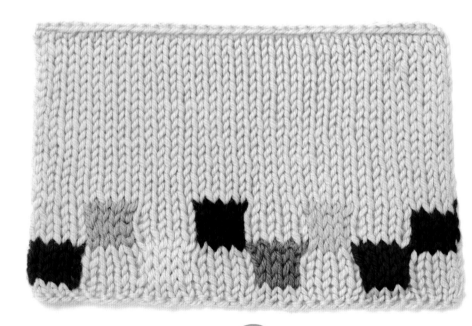

145

146

147 flowerbed

M1-p (make one purl)
Pick up horizontal thread between st just worked and next st, sl
it to LH needle, purl through the back loop.

(worked over 21 sts)

Note Sts for St st were picked up after edging was knit.

With A, cast on 21 sts.

Row 1 (WS) With A, P2, p2tog, p15, M1-p, p2.

Row 2 With A, Knit.

Row 3 With A, P2, p2tog, p15, M1-p, p2. Drop A and join C.

Row 4 With C, *Sl 1 wyib, k3; rep from *, end sl 1.

Rows 5 and 7 With C, *Sl 1 wyif, p3; rep from *, end sl 1.

Row 6 and 8 With C, *Sl 1 wyib, p3; rep from *, end sl 1.

Row 9 With C, *Sl 1 wyif, p3; rep from *, end k1. Cut C and pick
up A.

Row 10 With A, *K1, [insert RH needle into back of next st on
WS of work 6 rows below (last A row worked), pick up this lp
and place on LH needle, k tog with next st] 3 times; rep from *,
end k1.

Rows 11 to 20 Rep rows 1 to 10 using B for C.

Row 21 to 30 Rep rows 1 to 10 using D for C.

Rep rows 1–30.

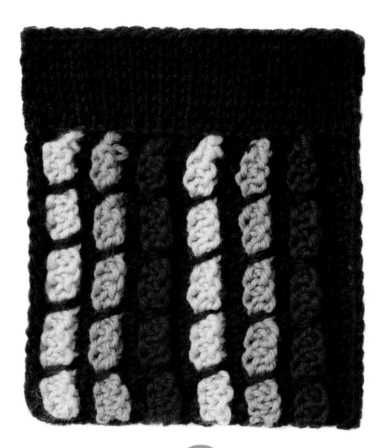

147

148 staggered stripes

(multiple of 4 sts)

With B, pick up and k evenly along edge. Purl 1 row.

Row 1 (RS) Knit with C.

Row 2 Purl with MC.

Row 3 *K2 A, k1 MC, k1 A; rep from * to end.

Row 4 P1 MC, p3 A; rep from * to end.

Row 5 Knit with MC.

Row 6 Purl with MC.

Row 7 Knit with C

Row 8 Purl with B.

Row 9 Knit with MC.

Bind off.

149 battleships

Note Sl all sts purlwise. On WS rows, bring yarn to front of work when slipping sts.

(multiple of 8 sts plus 3)

Cast on with A.

Row 1 (WS) Knit.

Row 2 With B, k1, *sl 1, k7; rep from *, end sl 1, k1.

Row 3 and all WS rows Knit the knit sts from previous row with same color and sl all the slipped sts.

Row 4 With A, k4, *sl 1, k1, sl 1, k5; rep from *, end sl 1, k1, sl 1 k4.

Row 6 With B, k3, *sl 1, k3; rep from * to end.

Row 8 With A, k2, *sl 1, k5, sl1, k1; rep from *, end k1.

Row 10 With B, k5, *sl 1, k7; rep from *, end sl 1, k5.

Row 12 Rep row 8.

Row 14 Rep row 6.

Row 16 Rep row 4.

Row 18 Rep row 2.

Row 20 With A, knit.

148

149

150 two-tier scallops

Colors A, B, C, D
(multiple of 16 st plus 1)
Cast on with A.

Row 1 (RS) With B, k1, *yo, [k1 tbl, p1] 7 times, k1 tbl, yo, k1; rep from * to end.

Row 2 K1, *p1, [p1 tbl, k1] 7 times, p1 tbl, p1, k1; rep from * to end.

Row 3 With C, k2, *yo, [k1 tbl, p1] 7 times, k1 tbl, yo, k3; rep from *, end last rep yo, k2.

Row 4 K2, *p1, [p1 tbl, k1] 7 times, p1 tbl, p1, k3; rep from *, end last rep p1, k2.

Row 5 With D, k3, *yo, [k1 tbl, p1] 7 times, k1 tbl, yo, k5; rep from *, end last rep yo, k3.

Row 6 K3, *p1, [p1 tbl, k1] 7 times, p1 tbl, p1, k5; rep from *, end last rep p1, k3.

Row 7 K4, *yo, [k1 tbl, p1] 7 times, k1 tbl, yo, k7; rep from *, end last rep yo, k4.

Row 8 K4, *p1, [p1 tbl, k1] 7 times, p1 tbl, p1, k7; rep from *, end last rep p1, k4.

Row 9 K5, *ssk 3 times, SK2P, k2tog 2 times, k9; rep from *, end k5.

Row 10 With A, purl.

Rep rows 1–10 once more.

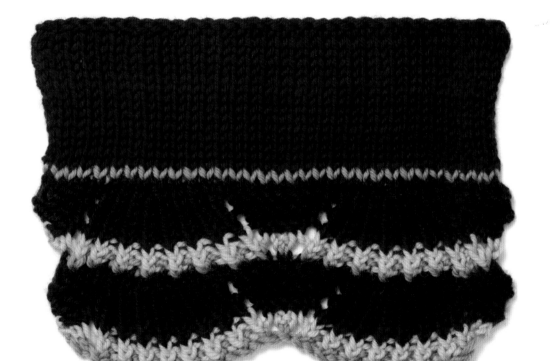

150

Stitch Key

☐ K on RS, p on WS

⊟ P on RS, k on WS

Color Key

 violet

■ plum

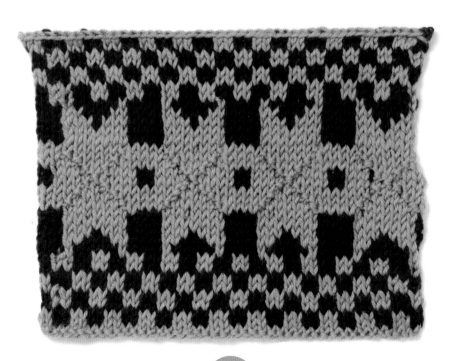

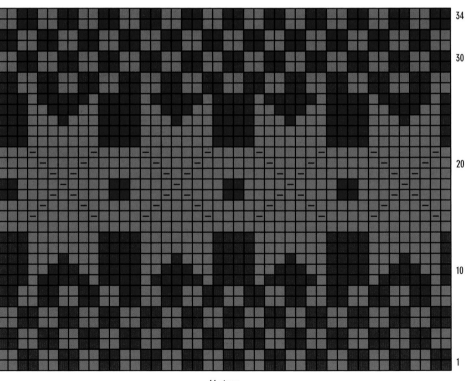

44-st rep

151

Lower Braid

(multiple of 2 sts)

Row 1 Pick up 1 st for each cast-on st, pick up and k * 1 st A, 1 st B; rep from *, carrying yarn on WS.

Row 2 P each st in same color as row 1, carrying yarns on RS and while working row place yarn used for each st over yarn used for previous st.

Row 3 K each st in same color as row 1, carrying yarns on RS and while working row place yarn used for each st under yarn used for previous st.

Bind off each st in same color as previous row.

Upper Braid

Row 1 (RS) *K1 A, k1 B; rep from * carrying yarn on WS.

Row 2 K each st in same color as row 1, carrying yarns on RS and while working row place yarn used for each st over yarn used for previous st.

Row 3 P each st in same color as row 1, carrying yarns on RS and while working row place yarn used for each st under yarn used for previous st.

Bind off each st in same color as previous row.

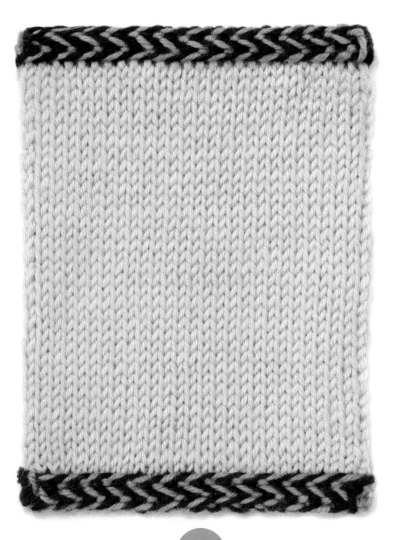

152

153 checks and balances

(multiple of 44 sts)

Rows 1, 5, 9, 13, 17 and 21 (RS) With A, *[wyib sl 1, k1] 5 times, k6, [wyib sl 1, k1] 5 times, k6, [wyib sl 1, k1] 3 times, k6; rep from * to end.

Rows 2, 6, 10, 14, 18 and 22 With A, *k6, [p1, wyif sl 1] 3 times, k6, [p1, wyif sl 1] 5 times, k6, [p1, wyif sl 1] 5 times; rep from * to end.

Rows 3, 7, 11, 15, 19 and 23 With B, *[k1, wyib sl 1] 5 times, k6, [k1, wyib sl 1] 5 times, k6, [k1, wyib sl 1] 3 times, k6; rep from * to end.

Rows 4, 8, 12, 16, 20 and 24 With B, *k6, [wyif sl 1, p1] 3 times, k6, [wyif sl 1, p1] 5 times, k6, [wyif sl 1, p1] 5 times; rep from * to end.

Rows 25 and 29 With A, *k10, [wyib sl 1, k1] 3 times, k10, [wyib sl 1, k1] 3 times, k6, [wyib sl 1, k1] 3 times; rep from * to end.

Row 26 With A, *[p1, wyif sl 1] 3 times, k6, [p1, wyif sl 1] 3 times, k10, [p1, wyif sl 1] 3 times, k10; rep from * to end.

153

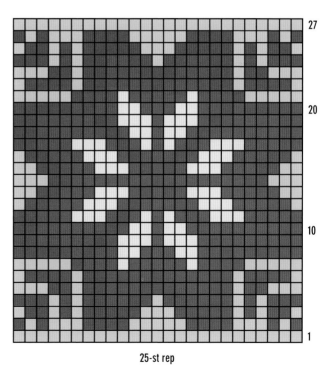

Color Key

▮ magenta

▮ rose

▯ pale pink

▯ ecru

27

20

10

1

25-st rep

154

Stitch Key

☐ K on RS, p on WS

⊟ P on RS, k on WS

Color Key

■ rose

☐ ecru

■ wine

☐ pale pink

■ violet

■ magenta

■ plum

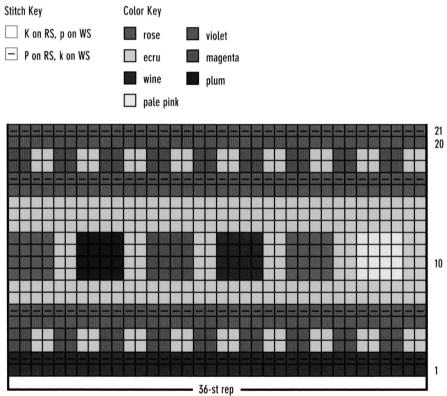

21
20

10

1

36-st rep

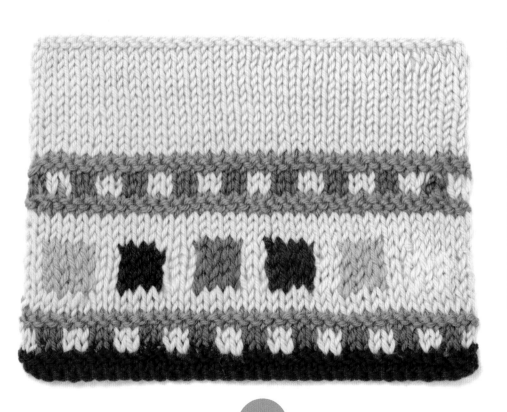

155

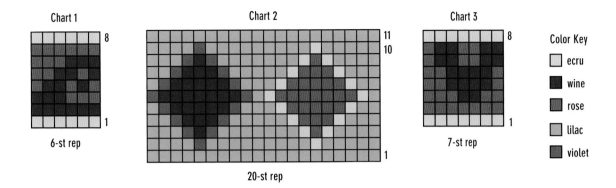

Chart 1

8

1

6-st rep

Chart 2

11
10

1

20-st rep

Chart 3

8

1

7-st rep

Color Key

☐ ecru
■ wine
■ rose
■ lilac
■ violet

156

157 pretty in pink

MB (Make Bobble) With A, k1, p1, k1 and p1 in 1 st, turn, p4tog,
turn, sl resulting st purlwise back to RH needle.

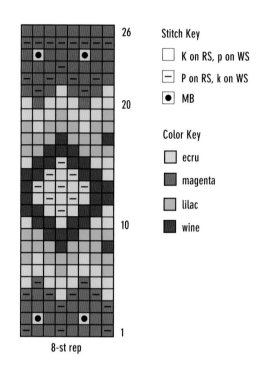

8-st rep

Stitch Key

☐ K on RS, p on WS

— P on RS, k on WS

● MB

Color Key

☐ ecru

■ magenta

■ lilac

■ wine

unusual

158 pompoms

1 With two circular pieces of cardboard the width of the desired pompom, cut a center hole. Then cut a pie-shaped wedge out of the circle.

2 Hold the two circles together and wrap the yarn tightly around the cardboard. Carefully cut around the cardboard.

3 Tie a piece of yarn tightly between the two circles. Remove the cardboard and trim the pompom.

Make pompoms and attach to piece evenly spaced.

159 basic fringe

For each fringe, cut 1 strand 6"/15cm long. Fold in half. On WS, insert crochet hook from front to back through each cast-on st and over folded yarn. Pull yarn through. Draw ends through and tighten. Trim yarn.

158

159

160 basic fringe II

For each fringe, cut 1 strand 4"/10cm long. Fold in half.
On WS, insert crochet hook from front to back through
piece and over folded yarn. Pull yarn through. Draw
ends through and tighten. Trim yarn. Work each fringe
in every other cast-on st.

161 chain-stitch fringe

For each fringe, cut 2 strands 6"/15cm long. Fold in half.
On WS, insert crochet hook from front to back through piece and
over folded yarn. Pull yarn through. Draw ends through and
tighten. Trim yarn. Space each fringe approx 1"/2.5cm apart.
With crochet hook, work chain sts of varying lengths up each
side above fringe.

unusual

160

161

162 easy weaving

Seed Stitch

Row 1 *K1, p1; rep from * to end.

Row 2 K the purl sts and p the knit sts.

Rep row 2.

(worked over an odd number of sts)

Row 1 Work in seed st.

Row 2 Working in seed st, work 2 sts, *yo, work 2 sts
tog, work 1 st; rep from * to end.

Row 3 Work in seed st.

Bind off. Weave ribbon through eyelet holes.

163 bobble band

(multiple of 4 sts plus 1)

Make Bobble (MB) [(P1, yo) twice, p1] in next st, turn, k5, turn,
p5, turn, ssk, k1, k2tog, turn, p3tog.

Row 1 (RS) K2, p1, k1, *MB, k1, p1, k1; rep from *, end k1.

Row 2 K1, *p1, k1; rep from * to end.

Row 3 K2, *p1, k1; rep from *, end k1.

Rep rows 2 and 3 twice more.

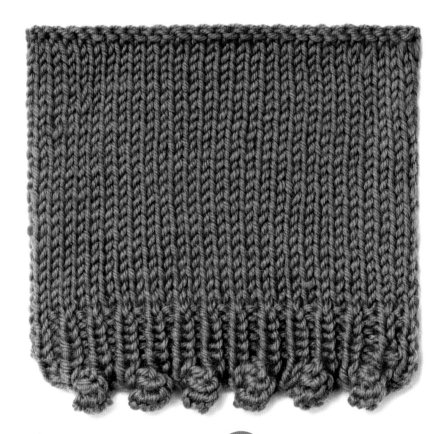

162

163

164 i-cord fringe

With dpn, cast on 3 sts.
*Slide sts to beg of needle without turning and k3; rep from *
until I-cord measures 3". Cut yarn leaving a 2"/5cm end. Place sts
on holder.
Cast on 2 sts, *k across 3 I-cord sts, cast on 1 st; rep from * until
all I-cords have been worked, cast on 2 sts.

165 mix it up

Along lower edge with dpn, pick up and k 5 sts from RS
along cast-on edge. Work in St st for 4"/10cm. Bind off.
Rep fringe randomly across edge and working different
lengths as desired.

unusual

164

165

131

166 tie the knot

With dpn, cast on 4 sts.
*Next row (RS) K4, do not turn. Slide sts to beg of needle to work the next row from RS; rep from * until I-cord measures 10". Thread I-cord in and out of lower edge at 2½"/6.5cm intervals and knot cord at front of work.

167 loop-di-loop

With dpn, *k4, turn and cont in St st on 4 sts until piece measures 4"/10cm from beg. Bind off, leaving a yarn end for sewing. With RS facing, join yarn in next st on LH needle; rep from * until all sts have been worked as loop fringe and bound off. Fold each fringe end to WS and sew bound-off edge to foundation row to form a loop.

166

167

174 easy embroidery

Cast on and work in garter st for 1"/2.5cm. Then work in St st until desired length.

Whip st around lower edge of garter st. Duplicate st every 3rd st on first row above garter st edging.

175 flower power

Seed Stitch

Row 1 *K1, p1; rep from * to end.

Row 2 K the purl sts and p the knit sts.

Rep row 2.

Rows 1, 2 and 3 Work in seed stitch.

Row 4 (WS) Knit.

Rows 5 to 11 Work in St st.

Row 12 (WS) Knit.

Embroider motif at lower edge.

174

175

176 bead it

Seed Stitch
Row 1 *K1, p1; rep from * to end.
Row 2 K the purl sts and p the knit sts.
Rep row 2.
1-st Bead
Sl 1 st wyif, place bead in front of this st, bring yarn to back ready to k next st.
Note Thread pearls onto yarn before beg.
(multiple of 6 sts)

Cast on and k 4 rows.
Row 1 Knit.
Rows 2 and 4 (WS) Purl.
Row 3 *K1, 1-st bead, k4; rep from * to end.
Rows 5, 6 and 7 Knit.
Rows 8, 9 and 10 Work in Seed st.
Rows 11, 12, 13 and 14 Knit.
Row 15 *K4, 1-st bead, k1; rep from * to end.
Rows 16 to 24 Rep rows 4 to 14.

177 beaded stripes

(multiple of 4 sts)
B1 Sl 1 wyif, place bead in front of st.
Note Thread beads onto yarn before beg.
Row 1 K1, p1, *B1, p1; rep from * to end.
Row 2 *K1, p1; rep from * to end.
Row 3 *K1, p1, k1 with pearl, p1; rep from * to end.
Rep rows 2 and 3.

176

177

178 pavé beads

(worked over an odd number of sts)

Rows 1 (RS) *K1, p1; rep from *, end k1.

Rows 2, 4 and 5 K the knit sts and p the purl sts.

Row 3 K1, p1, *pull pearl forward and sl 1 wyif so that pearl sits on RS in front of sl st, (pearl st on RS), p next st firmly; rep from *, end k1.

Row 6 P1, k1, *pull pearl forward and sl 1 wyib so that pearl sits on RS in front of sl st, (pearl st on WS, k next st firmly); rep from *, end p1.

Rep rows 1–6.

179 ruffled fringe

With RS facing, pick up and knit 1 st in every cast-on st at lower edge.

Next row K in front and back of each to double sts.

Next row *K2, M1; rep from *, end k2.

Next row *Cast on 4 sts, bind off 5 sts; rep from * until all sts have been worked.

178

179

180 beads and lace

(multiple of 14 sts plus 1)

S2KP Sl 2 sts as for k2tog, k1, pass 2 slipped sts over the k1 one at a time.

Place Bead (PB) First string beads onto working yarn. Work to position of bead, bring yarn to front (RS) of work, sl next st purlwise, slide bead along yarn so that it sits in front of st just slipped, then take yarn to back (WS) of work.

Row 1 (RS) K1, yo, p5, *p3tog, p5, yo, k1, yo, p5; rep from *, end p3tog, p5, yo, k1.

Row 2 and all WS rows Purl.

Rows 3 to 20 Rep rows 1 and 2.

Row 21 K4, k2tog, yo, k1, *k2, yo, SKP, k7, k2tog, yo, k1; rep from *, end k2, yo, SKP, k4.

Row 23 K3, k2tog, yo, k2, *PB, k2, yo, SKP, k5, k2tog, yo, k2; rep from *, end PB, k2, yo, SKP, k3.

Row 25 K2, k2tog, yo, k2, PB, *k1, PB, k2, yo, SKP, k3, k2tog, yo, k2, PB; rep from *, end k1, PB, k2, yo, SKP, k2.

Row 27 K1, k2tog, yo, k2, PB, k1, *k2, PB, k2, yo, SKP, k1, k2tog, yo, k2, PB, k1; rep from *, end k2, PB, k2, yo, SKP, k1.

Row 29 K2tog, yo, k2, PB, k2, *k3, PB, k2, yo, s2kp, yo, k2, PB, k2; rep from *, end k3, PB, k2, yo, SKP.

Row 31 K3, PB, k3, *k4, PB, k5, PB, k3; rep from *, end k4, PB, k3.

Row 33 K2, PB, k4, *k5, PB, k3, PB, k4; rep from *, end k5, PB, k2.

Row 35 K1, PB, k5, *k6, PB, k1, PB, k5; rep from *, end k6, PB, k1.

Row 37 K7, *k7, PB, k6; rep from *, end k8.

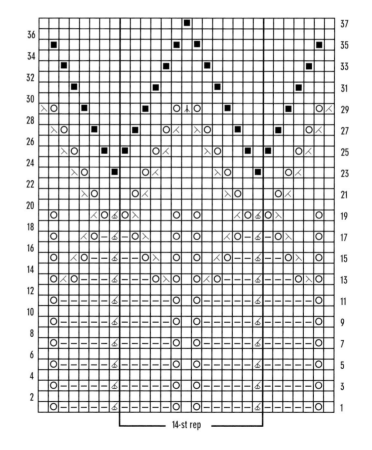

Stitch Key

☐	K on RS, p on WS
⊟	P on RS, k on WS
⟍	SKP
⟋	K2tog
⛏	P3tog
�	S2KP
○	Yo
■	Place Bead

14-st rep

180

140

crochet

181 chain

Work sc evenly along edge.
Working from left to right (or backwards), work as foll: *sc in 1 sc, ch 1 and skip 1 sc; rep from * to end.
Fasten off.

182 pretty picot

*Ch 5, slip 1 in next st; rep from *, end with slip 1 st in last ch.
Fasten off.

181

182

183 ripply ruffle

Work sc in back loop only of each bound-off st. Fasten off.
Rejoin yarn from RS and *work 2 sc and 1 hdc in 1 sc, ch 2,
sl st in next sc; rep from * to end.
Fasten off.

184 dewdrops

Row 1 (WS) Ch 2, 1 hdc in first st or space (for 2 hdc
group), *skip 1 st, work 2-hdc group in next st; rep from * to
end. Turn.
Row 2 Ch 1, sc in first hdc, *ch 3, sl st in first ch (picot), 1 sc
in each of next 4 hdc; rep from * to end.
Fasten off.

crochet

183

184

185 simple fringe

With WS facing, work along lower edge as foll: *Work 4 sl st, ch 10, sk 2 ch and work sl st into rem 8 ch; rep from * to end. Fasten off.

186 jellyfish

With RS facing and hook, join with a sl st in top right corner. Making sure that work lies flat, sc evenly along edge. Ch 1, turn.

Fringe row *Ch 40, sl st in next st, sc in next st; rep from * across. Fasten off.

185

186

187 twisted fringe

Place first st from needle on crochet hook, *ch 25, sl st into base (knitted) st, sl st into next stitch on LH needle; rep from * until all sts have been worked.

188 twisted fringe II

Row 1 *Work 1 sc approx 2 or 3 rows in from edge for spike sc, ch 4 and skip 2 sts (or space); rep from *, end spike sc in last st. Turn.
Row 2 *Work (1 sc, ch 2, 1 sc) in next sc, ch 2, (1sc, ch 4, 1 sl st, ch 4, 1 sc) in next sc for frill, ch 2; rep from *, end (1 sc, ch 2, 1 sc) in last st.
Fasten off.

187

188

189 tightly woven

Row 1 (RS) Ch 1, *1 sc in first st, ch 1, skip 1 st; rep from *, end 1 sc in last st. Do not turn.

Row 2 (reverse) *Ch 2 sl st in ch-1 sp; rep from * to end.

Row 3 Ch 1, *sc in ch-2 sp, ch 1; rep from * end sc in last st.

Rep rows 2 and 3 for 2".

Fasten off.

190 fishnet

With RS facing, join yarn, ch 5 sk 3, sc in next st, *ch 5 sk 3, sc in next st; rep from * to end.

Next row *Ch 5, sc in ch-5 sp, ch 5, sc in next sc; rep from * to end.

Fasten off.

191 wagon wheels

Work sc along edge. Turn.
Next row (RS) *Ch 3, sk 3 sc, 4 dc in next sc, ch 3, sk 3 sc, 1 sl st in next sc; rep from * to end.
Fasten off.

192 round and round

Row 1 (RS) Work sc evenly along edge. Turn.
Row 2 Ch 1, 3 sc in first 3 sc, *ch 3, 5 sc; rep from *, end 3 sc. Turn.
Row 3 Ch 1, 1 sc in first sc, *6 hdc in ch-3 lp, skip 2 sc, 1 sc in next sc; rep from * to end.
Fasten off.

crochet

191

192

193 double disk

Row 1 Sc evenly along edge.
Row 2 Ch 1, sc in next 6 sc, *2 sc, 3 sc in next sc, 16 sc; rep from * to end. Turn.
Row 3 Ch 3, skip 2 sc, 3 dc in next sc, ch 2, skip 2 sc, sc in next sc, *ch 2, skip 2 sc, 3 dc in next sc, [ch 2, skip 2 sc, sc in sc] twice, ch 2, skip 2 sc, 3 dc in center sc of 3 sc cluster, ch 2, skip 2 sc, sc in next sc, ch 2, skip 2 sc, 3 dc in next sc, ch 2, skip 2 sc, sc in next sc; rep from * around.
Fasten off.

194 eyelet picot

Work sc evenly along edge. Turn.
Row 2 (WS) Ch 3 (counts as first dc), *2 dc in next sc, 1 dc in next sc; rep from * to end. Ch 1, turn.
Row 3 (RS) Sc in first sc, *ch 4 skip next sc, sc in next sc, ch 1, skip 1 sc, sc in next sc; rep from * around.
Fasten off.

193

194

195 crochet scallops

Row 1 (WS) Work sc evenly along edge. Ch 1, turn.
Row 2 (scallop rnd) *Sc in first st, skip next sc, work 5 dc in next sc, skip next st; rep from *, end sc in last st.
Fasten off.

196 daisy chain

Work sc evenly along edge.
Row 1 Ch 3, skip 1 st, *2 dc in next st, ch 2, 2 dc in next st, ch 1, skip 3 sts; rep from *, end last rep with skip 1 st, dc in top of ch-3, turn.
Row 2 Ch 3, *work 7 dc in ch-2 space, 1 sc in ch-1 space; rep from *, end sl st in top of t-ch.
Fasten off.

195

196

197 wild roses

Row 1 (3 dc, 1 sc) in same space evenly along edge.

Row 2 Sl st along the top of all sts back to beg st. Turn.

Row 3 Skip 3 dc, *(1 sc, 3 dc) in sp between 3rd dc and sc of rnd 1; rep from *, end sc in last sp of last shell.
Fasten off.

198 rolling along

Ch 3 (counts as first dc), dc in each foundation ch around (OR dc in each st).

Ch 3, dc in each dc.

Scallop rnd Ch 1, *1 sc in same st as ch 1, skip 2 dc, work 7 dc in next dc, skip 2 dc; rep from *, end sc in last dc.
Fasten off.

197

198

3-hdc Cluster Yo, insert hook in next st, yo and through 2 loops, [yo, insert hook in same st, yo and through 2 loops] twice, yo and through all 4 loops on hook.

With RS facing and crochet hook, work 2 rows hdc evenly along edge. Ch 3, turn at end of last row.

Next row *Work 3-hdc cluster in next st, ch 3, sl st in next st, ch 3; rep from * to end. Fasten off.

199

200 broken windows

Row 1 Sc evenly along edge. Turn.

Row 2 Ch 5 (counts as 1 dc and ch 2), skip next 2 sc and work 1 dc in each of next 4 sc, *ch 2, skip 2 sc, work 4 dc; rep from * to end, turn.

Row 3 Ch 5, (counts as 1 dc and ch 2), skip 2 dc, *1 dc in next dc, 2 dc in ch-2 space, dc in next dc, ch 2, skip 2 dc; rep from *, end 1 dc in next dc, 2 dc in ch-2 sp, dc in 3rd ch of ch 5. Turn.

Row 4 Rep row 3 until desired length.

Fasten off.

201 wallpaper border

3-hdc Cluster Yo, insert hook in next st, yo and through 2 loops, [yo, insert hook in same st, yo and through 2 loops] twice, yo and through all 4 loops on hook.

With RS facing and crochet hook, work 2 rnds hdc evenly along edge.

Next rnd *Work 3-hdc cluster in next st, ch 1, skip 1 st; rep from * around.

Next rnd Work sc in top of each cluster and each ch-1 space.

Fasten off.

200

201

202 punch chain

Make a loop on hook and hold yarn at WS of piece, with punch-style crochet (punching yarn into fabric), *pull loop to RS at 2 rows from edge, work a chain punch st framing the inside of entire piece.

Work a zigzag st, working first just below the chain, then ch 2 and work punch sc in an angle above the chain, ch2; rep from *.

203 flower show

Ch 5, join with sl st to first ch to form ring.
Rnd 1 Ch 2 (counts as 1 sc), work 15 sc into ring, join with a sl st to beg ch.
Rnd 2 [Ch 4, sk 2 sc, sl st in next sc] 5 times, end last rep sl st in base of beg ch.
Rnd 3 In each ch-4 sp around work (1 sc, 3 dc, 1 tr, 3 dc, 1 sc), join with sl st to first sc.

Rnd 4 [Ch 5, sl st between next 2 sc (between petals)] 5 times, end sl st to base of beg ch.
Rnd 5 Ch 1, work (1 sc, 4 dc, 2 tr, 4 dc, 1 sc) in each ch-5 sp around, end sl st to beg ch.
Sew flowers evenly to garment.

202

203

204 renaissance lace

Work a row of sc evenly along edge.
Ch 1, turn.
Work 1 row more of sc , ch 1, turn.
Row 3 Sc in first sc, *ch 1, skip 1 sc, sc in next sc, dc in each of next 4 sc, sc in next sc, ch 1, skip 1 sc, sc in next sc; rep from * to end, ch 1, turn.
Row 4 *2 sc in next ch-1 sp, (sc, ch 3, sc) in next sp between sc and dc of previous row, sc in next sp between 2 dc, (sc, ch 3, sc) in next sp between 2 dcs, sc in next sp between 2 dcs, (sc, ch 3, sc) in next sp between dc and sc of previous row, 2 sc in next ch-1 sp; rep from * to end.
Fasten off.

205 rich ruffles

Work sc evenly along edge. Ch 1, turn.
Row 1 (WS) Sc in 1 sc, *sk next sc, (2 dc, ch 1, 2 dc) in next sc, sc in next st; rep from *, end sc in last sc. Ch 1, turn.
Row 2 Sc in 1 sc, *(2 dc, ch 1, 2dc) in next ch-1 sp, sc in next sc; rep from *, end sc in last sc. Ch 1, turn.
Row 3 Rep row 2 but do not turn. Working from right to left, work 1 backward sc in each sc and each dc.
Fasten off.

204

205

206 latticework

(multiple of 3 plus 2)

Row 1 Work sc evenly along edge. Turn.

Row 2 Ch 3, 1 dc in first st, *ch 1, skip 1 st, 1 dc in each of next 2 sts; rep from * to end, turn.

Row 3 Ch 3, 1 dc in each dc and each ch-1 space across, turn.

Rows 4 to 7 Rep rows 2 and 3 twice more.

Row 8 Ch 3, skip 1 st, *2 dc in next st, ch 2, 2 dc in next st, ch 1, skip 3 sts; rep from *, end last rep with skip 1 st, dc in top of ch-3, turn.

Row 9 Ch 3, *work 7 dc in ch-2 space, 1 sc in ch-1 space; rep from *, end sl st in top of t-ch.

Fasten off.

206

207 filigree

(multiple of 11 sts plus 10)

With WS facing, work sc evenly along edge. Ch 3, turn.

Row 2 Work 1 dc in first st, *ch 1, skip 1 sc, work 2 dc; rep from * to end. Turn.

Row 3 Work sc evenly in each dc and sp across. Turn.

Row 4 Ch 5 (counts as 1 tr and 1 ch), [work 1 tr, ch 1] twice into first sc, skip 4 sc, 1 sc in next sc, *ch 1, skip 4 sc, into next sc work [1 tr, ch 1] 5 times, skip 4 sc, 1 sc in next sc; rep from * to last 5 sc, ch 1, work 1 tr in last sc, ch 1, into same st as last tr work (1 tr, ch 1, 1 tr). Turn.

Row 5 Ch 1, 1 sc in first tr, *ch 2, in next sc work [1 dtr, ch 2] 4 times, skip 2 tr, 1 sc in next tr; rep from *, end by working last sc into 4th ch of ch-5. Turn.

Row 6 Ch 1, 1 sc in first sc, *ch 4, skip next sp, work 1 bobble into next ch-2 sp as foll: work 3 dc in ch-2 sp, working each dc until 1 loop rem on hook, yo and pull through all 4 loops on hook (1 bobble completed), [ch 3, 1 bobble in next ch-2 sp] twice, ch 4, 1 sc in next sc; rep from * to end.

Fasten off.

207

208 double decker

Row 1 Work sc evenly along edge. Turn.

Row 2 Ch 4 (counts as 1 dc and 1 ch), *skip 1 sc and work dc in next dc, ch 1; rep from *, end 1 dc. Turn.

Row 3 Ch 3, work 1 dc in each dc and in each ch-1 space to end, 1 dc in 3rd ch of turning chain. Turn.

Row 4 Rep row 2.

Row 5 Ch 4, work 1 dc in next dc, *ch 1, skip ch-1 space, work 1 dc in next dc; rep from * to end, 1 dc in 3rd ch of ch-4. Turn.

Row 6 Ch 1, work 1 sc in first dc, 1 sc in ch-1 space, 1 sc in next dc, *ch 3, skip next (dc and ch 1), work 1 sc in each of next 3 sts (counting each ch-1 space as 1 st); rep from * to end. Turn.

Row 7 Work 8 dc shell in each ch-3 loop and 1 sc in 2nd sc of the 3 sc of previous row.

Fasten off.

208

209 cobwebs

Row1 (RS) Work sc evenly along edge. Turn.

Row 2 Ch 3, 1 dc in first sc, *ch 2, skip 4 sc, (1 dc, ch 3, 1 dc) in next sc; rep from *, end last rep with skip 4 sc, 2 dc in last sc, turn.

Rows 3 and 5 Ch 3, 1 dc in first dc, *5 dc in ch-3 space; rep from *, end 2 dc in tip of ch-3, turn.

Rows 4 and 6 Ch 3, 1 dc between first 2 dc, *ch 2, (1 dc, ch 5, 1 dc) in 3rd dc of 5-dc group; rep from *, end ch 2, 2dc in last dc, turn.

Row 7 Rep row 3.

Row 8 Ch 3, sc in first dc, *ch 3, sc in 2nd dc of ch-5 group, ch 5, skip 1 dc, sc in 4th dc of 5-ch group, ch 3, sc in ch-2 space; rep from *, end last rep sc in last dc.

Fasten off.

209

Open Mesh Stitch

With crochet hook, chain 5".

Row 1 Sc in 2nd ch from hook and in each ch to end, ch 1, turn.

Work even in sc for 2 rows more, ch 4, turn on last row.

Next row Skip first sc, *dc in next sc, ch 1, skip 1 sc; rep from *, end dc in last sc. Ch 4, counts as first dc, turn.

Next row Dc in 2nd dc, *ch 1, skip ch 1-sp, dc in next dc; rep from *, end dc in 3rd ch of ch 4.

Rep last row until piece measures 4".

Fasten off.

Loop Fringe

Cut yarn 10" long. Fold each length in half and in half again, knot each doubled fringe in each ch 1-sp.

210

211 metro

Row 1 (WS) Ch 1, work 1 sc evenly along edge. Turn.

Row 2 Ch 1, work 1 sc in each sc. Turn.

Row 3 Ch 4, *skip 1 sc, dc in next sc, ch 1; rep from *, end dc in last st. Turn.

Row 4 Ch 1, work 1 sc in each dc and in each ch-1 space around. Turn.

Row 5 Work even in sc. Turn.

Row 6 Ch 1, *work 1 sl st in each of 2 sc, (sl st, ch 3, dc, ch 3, sl st) in next sc; rep from *, end 2 sl st in last 2 sts. Fasten off.

212 tiered scallops

Row 1 With WS facing, ch 1 and sc evenly along edge.

Row 2 Ch 3, 1 dc in first sc, *sc in next sc, skip 1 sc, 5 dc shell in next sc, skip 1 sc, sc in next sc, 5 dc shell in next sc; rep from *, end 3 dc (half shell) in last sc. Ch 1, turn.

Row 3 Sc in first dc, *5 dc shell in next sc, sc in 3rd dc of next shell; rep from *, end last rep sc in last dc. Ch 3, turn.

Row 4 Ch 3, 1 dc in first sc, *sc in 3rd dc of next shell, 5 dc shell in next sc; rep from *, end last rep 3 dc in last sc.

Row 5 Rep row 3 but fasten off after last sc.

211

212

213 loopy lace

Row 1 Ch 3, (1 dc, ch 2, 2 dc) in same sp as last sl st, *ch 6, skip next 4 sts, 1 sc in next st, ch 3, skip next st, 1 sc in next st, ch 6, skip next 4 sts, (2 dc, ch 2, 2 dc) in next st; rep from * to end. Turn.

Row 2 Sl st in next dc and ch 2-sp, ch 3, (1 dc, ch 2, 2 dc) all in same sp as last sl st, *ch 3, 1 sc in next ch-6 sp, ch 6, skip next ch 3-sp, 1 sc in next sc 6-sp, ch 3, (2 dc, ch 2, 2 dc) in next ch-2 sp; rep from * to end. Turn.

Row 3 Sl st in next dc and ch 2-sp, ch 3, (1 dc, ch 2, 2 dc) all in same sp as last sl st, *(1 tr, ch 3, sl st in top of tr — picot made) 11 times in next ch-6 sp, (2 dc, ch 2, 2 dc) in next ch-2 sp; rep from * to end.
Fasten off.

213

Row 1 (WS) Sc evenly along edge.

Row 2 Ch 3 (counts as 1 hdc and ch 1), skip 1 sc, * 1 hdc in next sc, ch 1, skip 1 sc; rep from *, end 1 hdc. Turn.

Row 3 Ch 4 (counts as 1 dc and ch 1), sc in same st, [1 dc, ch 1, 1 sc] in in each hdc. Turn.

Row 4 Ch 3 (counts as dc), 3 dc in ch 1 space, ch 1, sc in next ch-1 sp, ch 1, sc in same space as first sc, ch 1, *4 dc in ch to 1 sp, ch 1, [sc, ch 1, sc] in next ch-1 sp, ch 1; rep from *, end 4 dc. Turn.

Row 5 *Sc in first dc of 4 to dc group, ch 3, sl st in first ch (picot), [sc in next dc, work picot] twice, sc between next 2 sc, work picot; rep from * to end.

Fasten off.

214

215 hanging chad

With RS facing, work sc evenly across. Cut yarn.
Row 1 Join yarn and sc in 2nd ch from hook and in each ch to end—13 sc, turn.
Row 2 Ch 1, then working through back lps only, work 1 sc in each sc to end, turn.
Rows 3 and 4 Rep row 2.
Row 5 Ch 5, 1 sc in 2nd ch from hook, 1 sc in each of next 3 ch, then working through back lps only, 1 sc in each of next 9 sc, leave rem 4 sc unworked— 13 sc, turn.
Rep rows 2 to 5 for desired length.
Fasten off.

216 tri-dangles

Row 1 (WS) Ch 1. Work sc evenly spaced along edge. Turn.
Row 2 *Ch 8, sc in 2nd ch from hook, hdc in next ch, dc in next ch, tr in next ch, double tr in each of next 3 ch, skip next 4 sc, sc in next sc; rep from * to end. Fasten off.

crochet

215

216

217 chevron ruffle

Row 1 With RS facing, insert hook into edge, yo, draw through edge and lp on hook, ch 22, *secure ch with a sl st to edge approx ⅜" away from first point, ch 22; rep from * to end. Turn.

Row 2 Ch 4, insert hook in 5th ch of ch-22 lp and *work 1 sc in each of next 7 ch, 2 sc in next ch, 1 sc in each of next 7 sc, insert hook in 5th ch of next loop and rep from * in all of the ch-22 loops. At the end of the last group of sc, ch 4 and sl st into base of ch-22 loop. Turn. Sl st in the 4 ch just made to first sc.

Rows 3 to 10 Ch 1, insert hook in first sc, yo and draw a lp through, insert hook in 2nd sc, yo and draw a lp through, yo and draw a lp through all 3 lps on hook—dec made, *1 sc in each of next 6 sts, 3 sc in next st, 1 sc in each of next 6 sts, [insert hook in next sc, yo and draw a lp through] 3 times, yo and draw a loop through all 4 lps on hook; rep from *, ending with a dec of last 2 sc into 1 sc, turn.

Row 11 Work as for row 3 but with 2 sc in top of each point instead of 3 sc.

Fasten off.

217

acknowledgments

Special thanks to:

The Knitters:
Rebecca Fox
Charlotte Parry
Ann Jones Saxon
Valerie Seals
Elizabeth White

And also:
Lisa Buccellato
Lori Steinberg

double ruffle p. 36

All yarn provided by Cascade Yarns
1224 Andover Park East
Tukwila, WA 98188
cascadeyarns.com

Knitting needles on cover provided by Lantern Moon.
Lantern Moon knitting needles are currently available in four distinct wood varieties. Made entirely
by hand, they are the perfect tools for knitters. The design detail and hand finishing make these
needles as wonderful to work with as they are beautiful. Visit Lantern Moon online at
www.lanternmoon.com.

index

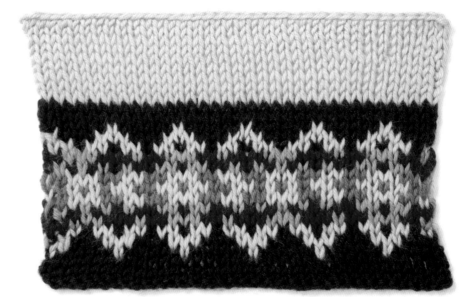

byzantine band p. 114

loop-di-loop p. 132

Complete your
STITCHIONARY
library with these titles

VOGUE KNITTING
STITCHIONARY
The Ultimate Stitch Dictionary from the Editors of Vogue Knitting Magazine
volume one
knit & purl

VOGUE KNITTING
STITCHIONARY 2
The Ultimate Stitch Dictionary from the Editors of Vogue Knitting Magazine
volume two
cables

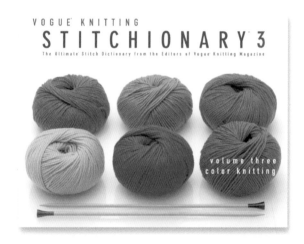

VOGUE KNITTING
STITCHIONARY 3
The Ultimate Stitch Dictionary from the Editors of Vogue Knitting Magazine
volume three
color knitting

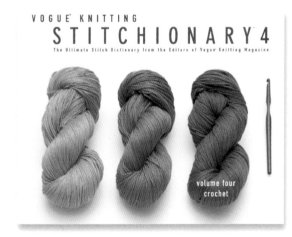

VOGUE KNITTING
STITCHIONARY 4
The Ultimate Stitch Dictionary from the Editors of Vogue Knitting Magazine
volume four
crochet

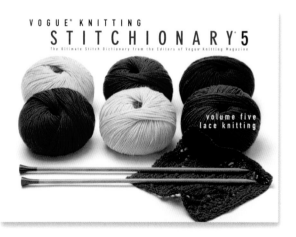

VOGUE KNITTING
STITCHIONARY 5
The Ultimate Stitch Dictionary from the Editors of Vogue Knitting Magazine
volume five
lace knitting